PREPARING A SUCCESSFUL BUSINESS PLAN

PREPARING A SUCCESSFUL BUSINESS PLAN

Rodger D. Touchie, MBA

Self-Counsel Press
(a division of)
International Self-Counsel Press Ltd.
Canada   USA

Printed in Canada.

First edition: 1989 Reprinted: 1990; 1991
Second edition: 1993 Reprinted: 1993; 1994; 1995; 1996; 1997
Third edition: 1998; 1998; 1999
Fourth edition: 2001

Canadian Cataloguing in Publication Data

Touchie, Rodger, 1944 —

Preparing a successful business plan

(Self-counsel business series)
ISBN 1-55180-371-2

1. Business planning. I. Title. II. Series.
HD62.7.T68 2001 658.4'012 C2001-911517-2

Self-Counsel Press
(a division of)
International Self-Counsel Press Ltd.

1481 Charlotte Road
North Vancouver, BC V7J 1H1
Canada

1704 N. State Street
Bellingham, WA 98225
USA

CONTENTS

SAMPLES

WORKSHEETS

PREFACE

I hope that you have opened this book because you are seriously considering a new business venture or rethinking an old one. Likely, you are either an entrepreneur or a project leader facing a new sense of responsibility and the need to articulate your ideas to those around you. Perhaps you have reached the point where you wish to chart your course and systematically review your expectations and assumptions about your business venture. You hold an ally in your hands.

However, before I get to the subject of business planning, let me establish one key point: you, the entrepreneur or project planner, the driving force behind a new business venture, are fighting tough odds. You are the foundation of the free enterprise system. It is your ambition, your personal initiative, your self-determination, your optimism, and your hard work that helps make this continent a land of opportunity.

You have picked a challenging road to walk through the quagmire of government bureaucracy, past more conservative colleagues. The time demands of your enterprise will be staggering and family and friends may not relate to your quest as you move into a world of prudent, occasionally insensitive money changers and professional advisers. Don't expect any favors from bankers, lawyers, accountants, consultants, or insurance agents. These specialists have their place in the scheme of things and the good ones can provide major assistance. Still, there is a danger in relying too much on their expertise. Beware of self-proclaimed experts who speak in vague generalities and seem preoccupied with covering themselves.

Enough scare tactics! A belief in yourself and your business can overcome all of these deterrents and will go a long way to helping you reach your goals, but it is best to enter the fray with your eyes open and with a sense of readiness.

There is only one way to prepare for the doubters and the cynics you will face and the followers and supporters you will lead. *You must plan.*

Preparing a Successful Business Plan won't meet all your current needs in your new (or changing) business, but it will set you firmly on the right track. It is designed as more than a "how to write" guide because a business plan is far more than a written report. I have tried to anticipate common problems and then stir your imagination in the solving of those problems.

To some extent, the scope of your business plan will depend on the expected size of your business. A two-person cabinet installation company is far less complex than a twenty-employee manufacturing plant, which in turn pales beside the challenge of implementing and distributing new technologies. In this book, I address issues as they apply to both small- and moderate-size ventures, and, therefore, it should provide guidance to business investments from $50,000 to $5,000,000.

Sound business planning cannot be done without some sense of vision. Much has been written in recent years about the changing demographics in North America and the impact of technology, especially the Internet, on future business. In this edition, I have attempted to provide specific insights into these issues, as well as promote the merits of innovation and the development of a planning mindset that can help your business rise above the norm.

Most discussions of changing economic forces as we entered the new millennium dwelt on demographic shifts and the impact of changing priorities among the aging boomer generation. Books on the subject became bestsellers as a subject usually left to academics became the hot topic at cocktail parties. Times were good, and "understanding the market" became as socially acceptable as "environmental awareness." Besides, having something other than interest rates, government fiscal policy, or unemployment as an influence on future market trends was a breath of fresh air.

In business planning, demographics is tied directly to the specific task of understanding and targeting your market, and hence developing a viable strategy to penetrate that market. To that end I have introduced some specific thoughts on the study of population trends in Chapter 4.

Technology is a different matter. More than thirty years ago, I wrote an MBA thesis on "The Economics of Integrating Computers and Communication Systems," a paper later printed in three parts by *Canadian Business Magazine*. At the time, few business planners even knew you could send binary business data down a telephone line. Words such as *modem, digital transmission,* and *networking* were in few vocabularies. A tape drive weighed a ton!

Entering the 1990s, "www" was unknown and "dot com companies" did not exist. John Naisbitt's bestselling *Megatrends* had not mentioned the Internet, and even the sequel, *Megatrends 2000,* failed to see the world beyond e-mail. So much for practical vision.

And then the world changed once more. On September 11, 2001, startling tragedies in New York and Washington DC shook the American psyche and magnified the impact that uncertainty and insecurity can have on the economy. Scenarios that had never been played out in any boardroom unfolded in a flash and the sudden change in buying patterns and travel plans brought many economic sectors to their knees.

These events have only tested the resilience of North America. Free enterprise may pause and step back to reassess, but then it will once more *prepare a plan* and move forward.

Today, technical awareness touches every aspect of business planning. Microchips, fiber optics, assorted new power sources, and the incredible data transmission grid that now covers the world all contribute to an infrastructure laden with new business opportunity. Technology and demographics deserve special emphasis in this time and place, but both must bow to the historic primary factor in business success — innovation.

In the early editions of this book, I have been remiss in not stressing the importance of a creative, knowledge-hungry mindset. As we enter a new century, the capacity to anticipate change, harness technology, and objectively measure both the risk and reward of the enterprise — the capacity to innovate effectively — will, more than ever, separate the successful from the unsuccessful. It will separate tomorrow's winners and losers.

Let's plan to win.

1
INTRODUCTION

Business planning is, above all, the application of common sense after anticipating the economic rewards of a specific enterprise.

a. WHAT IS A BUSINESS PLAN?

The term "business plan" has become a catchall phrase with different meanings to different people. Banks that release their own planning guidelines consider formal business loan applications to be synonymous with business plans. Venture capitalists see them as investment proposals, purely fund-raising documents. Corporate managers think of them in terms of departmental budgets and financial forecasts.

Your business plan will have elements of all of these things. But a business plan is much more than a written document. Too often, the production of the report, rather than the execution of the actual plan, becomes an end in itself. While the details that build a framework for success or failure are refined, the practicality often is ignored in the process. It is important to recognize that a business plan constitutes more than just a written document. *A business plan represents the dynamic process of planning and reviewing your business agenda over time, and it requires documentation in a format that allows regular updating in response to actual business conditions.*

If you set out to create a successful program, you must go many extra miles, far beyond the creation of a single-use document. You must establish an efficient means of altering course and readily modifying your overall plan. Commonly, business plans don't get updated because "it takes too much time." But revision takes too much time only if too little attention was paid in the first place to the recurring need for plan modifications. Not only now, but a year from now, you must know and be prepared to illustrate that your business plan is current.

This book will help you create a written plan and establish methods to assist you to regularly maintain that plan.

b. BEFORE THE PLANNING BEGINS

I would be suspicious of budding entrepreneurs or project leaders who delay the start of their venture until they completed a formal business plan. In practice, most self-starters have clear and often simplistic objectives that set them along the entrepreneurial path. Their initial focus *assumes* they will be successful, and they concentrate on refining their product or service rather than complicating their basic program with a formal business plan to the point where it never gets off the ground.

This focus is usually based on specialized knowledge within a specific field that allows the entrepreneur to target a product or service. For example, a computer programmer starting a software company should develop expertise in targeted applications and assess his or her ability to create specific programs for a known market before turning to the business plan. A sound justification for the economic purpose of the business must precede the formal planning process.

Outside of a classroom, there is only one stimulant that I have ever seen work to make an entrepreneur or project leader sit down and detail, within a single document, his or her business plan. That reason, to nobody's surprise, is money. It is either the money that you seek to raise, the money that you intend to make, or the money that requires authorization to spend that has likely driven you to this book for advice. Until the need for money arises, business plans often remain informal collections of memos, magazine articles, personal diaries, and mental notations.

For many people, the idea of systematically planning a business venture is not unlike public speaking. The thought of being exposed to criticism is intimidating. The challenge of actually writing a substantial document to be analyzed by professional financiers, boards of directors, fellow managers, and business associates is downright scary.

You may have good reason to be concerned about your inexperience and literary limitations, but there is no need to be intimidated. Just about anybody with common sense and a good idea can prepare a better-than-average business plan. The average plan prepared by a business before pursuing funding or other external support is often very poor. Professionals in enterprise development centers, banks, brokerage houses, and other financial institutions want to see a good business plan, but few of them expect a first-time entrepreneur to meet their standards.

This means that the plans that do meet the standard have two distinct advantages. First, they have surpassed expectation. Second, they are no longer competing in the financial marketplace with the plans of those who did not prepare.

If this approximates your starting point, you can use this book and the incorporated worksheets to focus your priorities and better understand the keys to successful business planning.

c. HOW TO USE THIS BOOK

This book is designed to assist you to successfully complete a project or program in your business that requires an investment of money to achieve economic gain. Chapter 2 considers basic issues that you must address before beginning the real work of business planning. Then, chapters 3 to 8 break business planning into six subjects or modules. I contend that the modular approach to gathering data is best for most planning exercises. In addition, planning modules are easier to maintain and update. These six chapters show how to develop the modules so you can begin to put the pieces of your plan into place. The final presentation of your formal business plan can easily follow the modules you prepare or be modified as the technical nature of your venture requires.

Worksheets are included in each chapter to assist you to collect the data you need for your business plan. Make as many copies of the worksheets as you need and modify them, if necessary, for your specific project. Accompanying each worksheet are some general guidelines and background on how to gather quality information.

The topics of presentation, style, and packaging of your business plan are looked at separately in chapter 9. The way your document looks, reads, and is presented exemplifies the level of professionalism that your business may attain and the quality of work that you will provide.

Although guided by the age-old KISS theory (keep it simple, stupid), a discussion of business planning must go beyond listing basic guidelines. Therefore, I have included in chapter 10 a discussion of sensible business philosophy and decision factors that enthusiastic entrepreneurs are inclined to overlook.

Many entrepreneurs have never seen an actual, formalized business plan. In Appendix 1, I have adapted a document that was originally commissioned by a private company to present a corporate business plan and help gain financing from institutional and noninstitutional investors. Reading this sample will help you establish a sense of direction in your plan, but it is atypical enough to show you that there is more than one way of doing things. Each business has its own quirks and personality, and the business plan should reflect that individuality. In fact, aspects of the sample plan may appear to contradict some of the book's recommendations, which emphasizes that this book is only a guide, and your own plan may be based on far different assertions that require different treatment.

If you run a small business, you need not be discouraged by the level of detail recommended. If you wear all of the management hats in a small operation, you can pare down your presentation accordingly.

Appendix 2 shows an example of some financial statements and Appendix 3 shows an operational memo used by another company; both these examples should prove useful references as you develop your own plan.

Some of the terms used throughout the text originate from the world of business communications; become familiar with this terminology as it can help establish an image of competence and business knowledge. As the driving force behind a business venture, you will be judged in conjunction with your business plan by all potential investors; your ability to incorporate business terms and language into your presentation will serve you well.

I have used the terms "product," "service," and "development" interchangeably in general description. Only in the detailed discussion of primary business purpose do I deal with the distinctive traits of the different business sectors. Manufacturing, service industry, distribution, and technology ventures should accordingly adapt the appropriate terminology.

Finally, I have written with one basic premise in mind: to help you demonstrate the ability to apply money wisely to a well-conceived business program and to communicate the expected results to a selected audience. The specifics of these issues, the amount of money, the actual goals, and the traits of the audience are details that you must explore.

The preparation of a sound business plan must go beyond the single objective of impressing the financier, however. When you finally toss this book in a corner for the last time, I hope that you will replace it with a business plan that will be the foundation of your internal management process for years to come. As your enterprise grows and the decisions become more complex, so will the planning exercise, but the basic framework should still be there and the concepts outlined here will continue to help direct you.

PLANNING IN THE WORLD OF TECHNOLOGY

Possibly the greatest challenges and opportunities in business will be directly related to your ongoing level of technology awareness. In the past 50 years, technology and the timing when applicants commit to it has become a dominant influence on business success.

Not only in the computer field but also in virtually all aspects of electronics, mechanics, and biochemistry have engineers and scientists made marvelous advances. However, for the business user, investment in technology is an ongoing battle. Buying into technical evolution at the wrong time or with the wrong supplier can quickly send a business to its knees. Be it a major investment that can directly impact company sales or cost efficiencies, a new computer for a department manager, or a new piece of equipment in a restaurant kitchen, if it changes your dependence from human factors to technology, I highly recommend that you weigh both the positives and negatives carefully.

Technology horror stories abound. Take the established printer who made a million-dollar decision in the early 1990s to accommodate the dynamics of a fast-changing desktop publishing industry. With both software and hardware capability changing at a rapid speed, the printer opted for new pre-production technology to handle a wide range of submissions via different technical mediums. When a competitor waited six months and hopped on the technology bandwagon one generation later, his pre-production system cost half as much and proved far more flexible. The problem was compounded when the first printer's pricing policy remained "bean-counter driven" and attempted to win back the money invested in passé technology. When the company started losing quotes, both market share and profits slipped badly.

Probably the single most important factor for business managers is the new reliance that must be placed on technologies in even the smallest of businesses. No longer can many business owners get at their mail with a letter opener or dig through a filing drawer to find a missing document. They must learn basic computer skills and e-mail techniques or they will perish. Timely information has always been critical to business success, and the less reliant one is on other people to be able to access information, the better a manager one will be.

This does *not* mean a manager requires extensive technical expertise. It *does* mean that you must develop an information system that accurately consolidates factual data and allows you to retrieve it if nobody else is around. It is incredible how often situations arise in our high-tech world in which executives, because they cannot personally access information, are at the mercy of a junior employee.

While information must be accessible, it must also be inaccessible. In many businesses, confidentiality and privacy are highly relevant to success. Creating electronic firewalls, establishing secure backup files, and isolating information files in limited-access databases are essential.

Another key factor in planning to harness technology is judging the implications that may come with retreat. By this I mean that you must be realistic about the number of technology companies that fail or the speed at which certain technical tools become obsolete. For those who decided to archive information on compact discs a decade ago, all has gone well. Other proponents of less successful storage devices and techniques have spent substantial time regrouping. When planning to introduce technology into your game plan or considering specific equipment options, measure both the potential of successful implementation and the consequences of failure.

2
GETTING STARTED: THE BASIC ELEMENTS OF BUSINESS PLANNING

There are five general considerations for all business planners to address as they set out to establish a formal business plan. This chapter explores five key questions:

(a) With whom is the planner trying to communicate?

(b) Who will participate in the planning process?

(c) What is the motivation for embarking on this venture?

(d) How do we get started?

(e) Can we define in a brief statement who we are and where we're going?

a. IDENTIFY YOUR TARGET AUDIENCE

Your written business plan is a document of communication. It is a message from you, using a traditional and acceptable medium, aimed at your target audience. Both the nature of your message and the medium are affected by your knowledge of your receiver. *The most underestimated step in preparing a business plan is establishing a reasonable knowledge of the target audience.*

For internal project plans, when you know precisely whom the report is aimed at (usually an executive decision-maker), evaluating and understanding the quirks of your audience is relatively easy. But even in this case, don't overlook the obvious. Once, when commissioned to develop "a total, all inclusive, five-year marketing plan" for a technology company, I sought direct input from four senior executives to identify their personal biases and assess their estimates of what the company and its absentee president were actually looking for. Weeks later, from a mass of drafts, spreadsheets, and data, I completed a slick-looking, well-illustrated document. When one of the senior executives first saw it, he smiled knowingly.

"Looks great," he said. "Too bad our president has the attention span of a mosquito. He's never read more than a two-page memo in his life."

I had failed to know my real audience.

If you are preparing your plan for a general audience, you need to do your homework. Fund-raising documents aimed at the institutional market are often the hardest to create because the unknown audience is a faceless horde of financiers in formal business attire.

There is something that can help you through this procedure enormously: the Target Audience Profile. Use the guidelines below and summarize your findings on Worksheet #1. You can use the information you gather in your first letter of introduction to pending financiers. This fact-finding process combined with an attention-getting letter (see Sample #1 in chapter 9) can help get you on the right track.

Using Worksheet #1: The Target Audience Profile

Consider the case of Mr. H., a former traveling salesman, intent on finding a way to spend less time on the road. Over the years, he perfected a new family board game. He took his game to the manager at his local bank with the idea of discussing financial backing. Like many budding entrepreneurs, he was shocked to find a disinterested manager who politely informed him that the bank was not in the investment business but the lending business and it might provide a loan in the form of a second mortgage on Mr. H.'s small home if he exhibited a track record of cash flow appropriate to servicing the loan. Of course, if Mr. H. gave up his sales job to pursue his venture, he could not demonstrate a secure income and would likely not meet loan qualification standards. Mr. H. was not going to get any help or sympathy from the banker.

Mr. H. had learned two things: banks do not provide risk equity financing and bankers can make a lousy audience.

Mr. H. had done a lot of groundwork on his project but made the big mistake of thinking that the game would sell itself. When he recognized this,

WORKSHEET #1
TARGET AUDIENCE PROFILE

TARGET'S NAME: ____________________

POSITION: ____________________

ADDRESS: ____________________

COMPANY: ____________________

TELEPHONE: __________ FAX: __________ REFERENCE: __________

SOURCES:

1. Name: ____________________ Telephone: __________
2. Name: ____________________ Telephone: __________
3. Name: ____________________ Telephone: __________

1. Target's personality and business traits: ____________________

2. Advisers' names: ____________________

3. Investment criteria: ____________________

4. Traditional level of support (financial and management): ____________________

5. Other investments: ____________________

6. Background on previous investment decisions: ____________________

7. Was business plan important to past investment decisions? ____________________

8. Second-round financial support history: ____________________

Mr. H. began work on the profile of his audience by questioning his actual needs and wants. He knew he needed $150,000, but he did not know where to get it.

Following are the questions he asked himself and the answers he developed:

Q: Do I want one big partner or six small partners?

A: Preferably one unless I must surrender more than 50% of the venture to secure the money.

Q: What is the minimum personal share of the company I want to retain?

A: Control is very important. Profit sharing should equate with investment, but I should retain full management.

Q: How can I maintain control if I have minimal money to invest?

A: Separate operating control from profit sharing. Have two classes of stock or a form of profit sharing debt.

Q: How much time and money can I invest to raise money?

A: Time is easier than money. I cannot afford personal travel outside my current sales territory.

Q: Who knows where money is?

A: Accountants, lawyers, financial advisers, stockbrokers, business managers, bankers, and fund raisers.

Q: Do I have any personal contacts who "know money?"

A: Enough to get me started.

After a week of general inquiries, Mr. H. drew up a list of 15 names ranging from a wealthy widow to the president of a local steel company. He then put his current employer at the end of the list. (Your employer may offer a special situation which I discuss later.)

Mr. H.'s short list of 15 candidates had only one thing in common: they were all known investors with a track record of backing local winners. Mr. H. then sought basic information about each name on his list from three different sources. Each source had a different relationship to his target. He wanted to understand each person's decision-making process, any unique likes and dislikes in business habits, who the key advisers were, and who each investor had backed before. He paraphrased his findings on Worksheet #1.

You need to use the same process to identify your audience. Ask yourself the key questions about your investment needs, as Mr. H. did, to isolate possible interested parties. Then find out as much as you can about your audience by contacting different sources: the people nearest to your target and those that know his or her business habits.

For example, Source 1 might be the executive assistant, secretary, or other staff support person of your target. A direct phone call to verify name, title, and mailing address of the target can provide you with the opportunity to ask questions about personality, business traits, and who your target's advisers are (from whom you can get further sources). You might try questions like these:

(a) "I am preparing a business report to deliver to Mr. Target and we want it to meet his needs and suit his general reading habits. You probably know his taste better than anybody, and I would really appreciate some of your insight, Ms. Jones, so that I can format this properly."

(b) "Before completing this for your employer, Ms. Jones, I wanted to review some of the details with some of his advisers. Whom do you feel would be the best single contact to fill in some specifics on Mr. Target's investment criteria?"

The answers to the first question might tell you that Mr. Target reads only two pages a week and you would be wasting your time sending a detailed document to him. Ideally, the answers to the second question will lead you to the best person to provide the information for sections 3, 4, and 5 on Worksheet #1. If you are stonewalled by a tight-lipped secretary at this point, do not despair. At the very least, you should be able to get the names of the company's accountant and members of the board of directors.

Source 2 should be the adviser or confidant of your target. When you first contact this person, it is important to be open and candid. The only thing to guard against is the unfortunate compulsion of many advisers to protect their chief from "external beggars." However, if you introduce yourself with self-confidence and a sense of purpose and set a tone of control at the same time, you shouldn't have any trouble overcoming the source's reluctance to talk to you.

You might say something like this:

"Hello, Mr. Smith. I'm preparing a business plan and investment proposal for Mr. Target and his office indicated that you might help with some input to help expedite the process. Could you outline Mr. Target's general investment criteria so I can confirm that we are on the right track?"

Use this approach both to send a message of respect and find out how involved Mr. Target likes to get in his investments. "We are hoping to develop a sound group of external expertise on a board of directors and I wanted to know if either you or Mr. Target would be inclined to commit some time at that level if we came to an investment arrangement."

Once you know how involved your potential investor likes to be, then get the names of people who have experienced your target as a shareholder. "I know that the Target Group has made similar investments with small companies and I am curious about your experience. Could you describe some of the good and the bad?"

Source 2 contacts are more readily available than you may think. These people generally expand their goodwill base by being a contact point for people who have a potential business relationship. They owe their success to their own networking ability. Many accountants and lawyers recognize long-term personal rewards from helping to bring "clients" together. Other professional directors are valuable to companies because they bring new, interesting business proposals to the senior management.

Source 2 contacts can be found at Board of Trade luncheons, professional seminars, and on executive golf courses. If the more direct method described above doesn't work, you may have to undertake the time-consuming task of "trolling for cash." Hours and days can be devoted to slowly dangling the bait of a potentially lucrative deal in a sea of professional networkers. Remain open to a finder's fee and plan the best locations to meet Source 2 candidates. In general terms, let them help define ideal targets.

Often, you will end up paying for this contact. However, I recommend that any payment be made only if a deal is consummated. Often payments can be indirect. For example, an accountant might be precluded by his or her professional guidelines from taking a direct concession. That accountant might, however, rightly expect that he or she be appointed as the external accountant to the new venture or be appointed to the board.

By extending Source 2 conversations to the topic of similar investments, you should be able to derive names of a few entrepreneurs, from which you can draw Source 3: an entrepreneur who has gone down this same road.

When you contact Source 3, as is the case with Source 2, it is better to ask the questions person to person. Call the entrepreneur for a meeting, preferably at his or her office, or offer to buy him or her lunch. Ask questions like the following:

(a) "How did you, Ms. Entrepreneur, attract Mr. Target to invest in your business?"

(b) "Did you present him with a complete plan and, if so, what were the key aspects that sold him on your business?"

(c) "What is your relationship with Mr. Target and would you expect him to maintain his pro rata equity position if you do another round of expansion financing?" (In other words, if Target now owns 20% of equity, would he contribute 20% of future required funding rather than dilute his percentage of ownership.)

Consolidate your notes onto Worksheet #1 for each of your key candidates. By the time you finish this exercise, you will have a good idea of whom your plan will be written for. If you have time for only one source, try to isolate a Source 3 candidate. The only caution is that such a source may see you as a competitor for your target's money and, as a result, not cooperate fully.

Previously, I suggested that you consider your current employer as a potential financial backer. Obviously, whether or not you feel comfortable doing this depends on your relationship and the nature of the company. Many larger companies have become very receptive to employees with an entrepreneurial spirit; likewise, smaller companies are quickly recognizing the value of this unique commodity.

I place employers at the end of the target list, although not because they are unlikely candidates. However, when you go to an employer with an investment proposal or business plan, I think it is prudent to know all of your external options — especially if there are any competitive overtones. If you choose this course and see a reasonable chance of a positive response, deal directly with the corporate decision-maker. Going through regular channels will usually only muddy the waters. You want to discuss this issue entrepreneur to entrepreneur.

b. THE MODULAR PRESENTATION TECHNIQUE

All business plans incorporate the same standard elements:

(a) The Executive Summary

(b) The Company and its Product (or Service)

(c) The Marketing Plan

(d) The Financial Plan

(e) The Team Profile

(f) Concluding Remarks

As a whole, the business plan attempts to relate the intended business to its position within an existing business environment. To accomplish this end, it is essential that you apply self-discipline in your corporate planning. One of the most effective means of doing this is to adopt a modular approach to business planning which can assist the fulfillment of your business objectives for years to come.

As I discuss later, the actual editing of the business plan document should be the work of one person, but modular planning encourages team input from managers responsible for specific functions. It also helps the project leader keep the contributors focused within their areas of expertise rather than send groups off on tangents unrelated to the task at hand.

Each module is derived from parameters provided by the corporate or project leader and is developed by a team of a few people involved in the venture. In small ventures, one person may wear all or most of the managerial hats and play an active role in developing all the modules.

The Company and its Product (or Service), the Marketing Plan, and the Financial Plan are handled differently from the other three modules because before you can begin work on them, you need to isolate the contributors to these and identify early goals and objectives. (Once you have done this, you will also have laid the groundwork for completing the Team Profile module.) Use Worksheet #2 to help you develop these three individual module teams, their goals, and guidelines. (You will want to copy the worksheet to use for each of these three modules.)

As the venture coordinator, you must be prepared to define your mandate and provide a reasonable sense of direction. The human chemistry and experience of your planning group will dictate the precision of your preliminary guidelines to each team. Do not be surprised if people do not respond well if you allow too much free thinking. Intuitively, modern managers want freedom to "run with the ball," but in practice, a group with limited experience will often fumble it.

If you are a lone entrepreneur looking in a mirror thinking "I am the team," do not despair. Modular planning is also meant for you. Your advantage is that you will not face the delays and posturing common to committee members. The weakness is that investors often don't like the thought that they must rely on one person for success.

Using Worksheet #2: Selecting Module Teams and Goals

For each of the three modules (the Company and its Product, the Marketing Plan, and the Financial Plan), identify those people you want on the team. You can either identify the players by name or job title. Identify the key financial, marketing, production, research, and administrative people as well as active corporate directors who might influence the planning process. Also list other individuals whose input you respect in the fields of product development or production (service development or management in the case of a service company) and marketing and sales. In finance you may want to involve an independent accounting firm, but this can prove to be expensive and diversionary unless you've got the right person.

Worksheet #2 is laid out so that you can summarize the main reason each individual is included. Space for a maximum of five contributors per team is allowed. Committees larger than this get unwieldy. My personal preference is three people in most cases. Remember team players must complement each other. It serves little purpose to include similar personalities or talents at this level. Collectively the team can sort out their individual tasks. Then, each team member can enlist specific support resources away from the planning table in line with their designated responsibilities. They can get input from their peers and staff and review the merits of different options. Ideally, they will select, recommend, and be prepared to defend the best of these options.

At this stage, you should set general guidelines; nothing should be cast in stone. For example, let's assume that you intend to have three or four people develop each module. Call them together, explain the procedure, and describe their roles. Emphasize that the senior managers will inherit the responsibility for quarterly or semi-annual updates of the planning parameters and that the process they are about to enter will be a basic management tool for years to come. That should get everybody's attention.

Start with the financial team. You need to achieve a consensus on the financial scope of your business so that you have a starting point for your production and marketing people. The chair of your financial team should be your senior financial executive (or you if you are controlling the purse

WORKSHEET #2

SELECTING MODULE TEAMS AND GOALS

Finance ❑
Product ❑
Marketing ❑

	NAME/POSITION	REASON FOR INCLUSION	TEAM ROLE
1.	______________	______________	______________
	______________	______________	______________
	______________	______________	______________
	______________	______________	______________
2.	______________	______________	______________
	______________	______________	______________
	______________	______________	______________
	______________	______________	______________
3.	______________	______________	______________
	______________	______________	______________
	______________	______________	______________
	______________	______________	______________
4.	______________	______________	______________
	______________	______________	______________
	______________	______________	______________
	______________	______________	______________
5.	______________	______________	______________
	______________	______________	______________
	______________	______________	______________
	______________	______________	______________

OBJECTIVES:

INTERMODULAR PRIORITIES:

1. (a) Finance must provide product team: ______________
   (b) Finance must provide marketing team: ______________
2. (a) Production must provide finance team: ______________
   (b) Production must provide marketing team: ______________
3. (a) Marketing must provide production team: ______________
   (b) Marketing must provide finance team: ______________

strings and are financially adept). One member must be familiar with a computerized spreadsheet package and have access to a computer. You likely have some definite preconceptions about costs, expected production levels, pricing, sales, capital investment, staffing requirements, facility rental, and equipment needs. Summarize these on the worksheet under the heading "Objectives" so you can toss them on the table and sift through the logic behind your estimates.

When setting financial objectives, avoid specific sales goals that are meaningless. Think more in terms of basic capital investment requirements. State all limitations including the known available funding level and any imposed constraints on further equity and debt financing. Seek out industry financial data that sets reasonable specifications for gross profit margins, operating expenses, and selling and promotion costs, and relate your business strategy accordingly. For example, if your intent is to go after higher volume by sacrificing profit margin, include this in your early financial objectives.

After you have completed the worksheet for the financial plan, you can start over with the production and marketing module teams. It is the production team's job to deal with the supply side of the equation. The mandate of the production group is to clearly detail what is necessary to ensure your ability to deliver quality and present clear information on your fixed and variable productions costs to operate at a variety of production levels.

The makeup of this team will depend on two critical elements: the technical level of your product or service and the complexity of the production process. Many development companies make the mistake of relying on their "inventor," the product development genius, as their primary product adviser. Solving technical product development issues involves a totally different perspective than mass producing units once the technical criteria are set.

Even the largest technical companies clearly distinguish between product development and production input. Ideal members of the product team cover both of these fields. A third member might have marketing expertise as no serious product decisions can be finalized without some input that represents the perspective of the end user.

The marketing module team must identify the potential customer base and verify the existence of a demand at prices consistent with revenue forecasts. It should outline what must be done to ensure a positive consumer response to the product and relate a viable product price range to consumer demand.

If possible, the marketing team members should include both a trained marketing strategist and a sales manager. Sales people who live in the field can bring a valuable perspective to the planning table and introduce critical issues. In most cases, the senior marketing person on this team should also be part of the product team. The company's senior financial officer is ideal to round out this group and provide number crunching and cost analysis skills.

Choosing team members is not enough. Worksheet #2 allows room for you to summarize the participants' roles. What is it that you expect of each individual? You may wish to expand on the summary in this worksheet and meet with team members individually to discuss their roles. This process will help overcome any uncertainties; people generally want to know what is expected of them.

You can outline why their expertise is important to the module committee and give examples of how you expect it to be applied. Harder to specify are the levels of creativity, cooperation, and focus that you expect.

Ultimately, the first job of your chosen team is to review the defined objectives and conduct a self-assessment of their combined abilities to meet your expectations. If the individuals and their roles don't line up with the objectives, the team must acknowledge this and fill those gaps accordingly.

The bottom section of the worksheet will help you anticipate the key data that each module team must provide to their counterparts early in the planning process. This interaction should quickly isolate any problem areas. For example, if the finance team tells the production team that the company will not be able to raise more than $1 million and production needs $2 million in equipment to operate efficiently, you have quickly isolated a key problem. If marketing concludes that the end consumer will not pay more than $10 per unit regardless of quality, then finance and production must evaluate the likelihood of producing on a cost-effective basis to achieve reasonable profit margins. These issues exemplify why participation by some team members on more than one module's team can be important.

Getting your plan started is much easier when your business is contemplating expansion than it is in a start-up situation. Purists in planning may disagree and condemn these early presumptions as restrictive on the planners. I disagree. It's your business and you have a responsibility to provide guidance, rules, and expectations. If you have a clear understanding of how you wish to operate or the critical production level needed to optimize average unit cost, then you should set those levels as production goals and sales targets right up front. Planning committees (like all committees) can go off on tangents very quickly, and you must make sure they stay focused.

c. UNDERSTANDING THE RISK/REWARD RELATIONSHIP

Any new business project has a high risk attached to it. While the entrepreneur is always optimistic about the chance of success, most readers of the business plan would rather err on the side of caution. If they recommend participation in your venture, it is because the potential reward outweighs the attached risk. Risk/reward evaluation is the foundation of financial analysis and this will be the basis on which your business plan is judged.

Worksheet #3, Exploring the Risks, and Worksheet #4, Exploring the Rewards, are aimed at gathering information that is vital to a good Executive Summary. This, arguably, might be described as putting the cart before the horse. You may ask how you can summarize what you have not yet written. My answer is, "How can you plan a document if you do not contemplate the content of your ultimate message?"

The Executive Summary is the single most important module of your business plan. The impact of this section on the reader will establish the level of enthusiasm toward your project. Because it summarizes all key points related to the financial feasibility of your business, it is never too early to contemplate the scope and factors that must be considered.

To some extent, the message of all Executive Summaries is the same. They state that money invested in the proposed business activity will yield an attractive return on investment. They detail the exact funding required and summarize the financial structure of the required investment or budgeted cash flow. They estimate an annual return on investment. They identify the unique factors that make this venture different from others. They strive to capture the imagination of the reader and anticipate the key questions that will arise in his or her mind. Above all, they answer the key issues related to pending risk and potential reward.

Every time an investor parts with a dollar, he or she runs the risk of never seeing it again. The acceptability of risk-taking varies from source to source, but all will agree that the best way to reduce risk is to increase knowledge of the potential investment. The business planner can substantially broaden financial sources by anticipating the perceived risks and reducing or eliminating unknown factors.

By completing Worksheet #3, you will put yourself in the position of the financier you must ultimately attract.

Willingness to expand the acceptable risk is dictated by the expected rewards to be gained. Investor rewards come in the form of dividends or capital gains, but the potential is measured indirectly. The rewards that the business will gain by applying those dollars are of primary interest to the investor. Will the reward of investment be a better product, more production capacity, broader market potential, faster customer response, or more efficient administration? Use Worksheet #4 to help set the tone for expressing yourself in terms of rewards.

Using Worksheet #3: Exploring the Risks

If the Executive Summary does only one thing, *it must describe a risk/reward relationship* that meets the criteria of the reader. Otherwise the entire effort is for nothing. For this reason, the emphasis of specific Executive Summaries varies with the audience and the same business plan may be introduced to different parties with a tailored Executive Summary. However, at this stage, your goal is to set ball-park expectations and assess whether you are going to be able to tell the audience what it wants to hear.

To complete the first half of the worksheet, seek out representative financiers in your community. Remember that the exercise here is to collect data on the perceived rewards and risks associated with your overall business. Arrange meetings with financial people on the understanding that you are starting a business and interviewing prospective financial services that you expect to require in the future. Be prepared to briefly describe your product and general business program. Encourage discussion and listen carefully. Encourage them to express their concerns. Can you clarify any points to help reduce uncertainty?

Try to take the conversation beyond the polite stage to get true impressions. If necessary, introduce risk into the discussion directly. Ask what they see as the major risks of the business. After your interview, fill out Worksheet #3 and consider how you can reduce the perceived risk.

Professional investors will likely want a minimum annual return of 30% on invested capital. If your business is extremely risky, this percentage may be higher. Find out the techniques that are preferred to minimize risk. Some financiers will invest only in capital-intensive projects where they secure a first charge against tangible assets acquired with their funding. If your business fails, they liquidate those assets to recover some of their investment. Others will suggest preferred shares that rank ahead of common shares in a

WORKSHEET #3
EXPLORING THE RISKS

1. PRODUCT COMPLEXITY

Apparent risk perception: ____________________

____

Action possible to reduce: ____________________

____

2. PRODUCT LIFE

Apparent risk perception: ____________________

____

Action possible to reduce: ____________________

____

3. PRODUCTION UNKNOWNS

Apparent risk perception: ____________________

____

Action possible to reduce: ____________________

____

4. LEGAL PROTECTION

Apparent risk perception: ____________________

____

Action possible to reduce: ____________________

____

5. DISTRIBUTION STRUCTURE

Apparent risk perception: ____________________

____

Action possible to reduce: ____________________

____

6. COMPETITION

Apparent risk perception: ____________________

____

Action possible to reduce: ____________________

____

7. PROMOTABILITY

Apparent risk perception: ____________________

____

Action possible to reduce: ____________________

____

WORKSHEET #3
Continued

8. PRICE SENSITIVITY

Apparent risk perception:____________________

Action possible to reduce: ____________________

9. CUSTOMER FINANCIAL STABILITY

Apparent risk perception:____________________

Action possible to reduce: ____________________

10. EXPOSURE TO INTEREST RATES

Apparent risk perception:____________________

Action possible to reduce: ____________________

11. ____________

Apparent risk perception:____________________

Action possible to reduce: ____________________

12. ____________

Apparent risk perception:____________________

Action possible to reduce: ____________________

13. ____________

Apparent risk perception:____________________

Action possible to reduce: ____________________

14. ____________

Apparent risk perception:____________________

Action possible to reduce: ____________________

profit-sharing plan. Convertible debt is the popular choice of many investors who want short-term protection against the down times but long-term equity participation if the project succeeds.

Investors will attach a high risk on any technical business that they do not understand. Evaluate your ability to reduce risk perception by educating your audience and removing doubts. What is the success ratio in your industry? Are there tangible examples of success that parallel your program? How important is management experience in the eyes of the audience and how do you stack up? Will you have to quote Norman Vincent Peale's *Enthusiasm Makes the Difference* to offset this problem or recruit a manager who brings maturity to the team?

Does your target audience question the market's acceptance of your product? Is independent market research and confirmation of demand required to remove doubts? How critical is your promotion program to the achievement of sales? How established is the competition? If you are competing against huge, successful corporations, can you verify for the investor that you will even be able to enter the game?

Are there tax incentives or government protections that reduce the risk? What success/failure ratio is built into the investors' overall program?

Must your potential investors meet standards of "due diligence" as a part of their investment process? This reflects a level of research often demanded of public company executives, lawyers, and accountants who are charged with advising clients or shareholders on their investments. Due diligence is an intangible standard of precaution that professionals must exhibit if they are to avoid personal liability should your venture fail. Often this precaution takes the form of an independent technical evaluation or market study of your business program commissioned by the investor. The findings of that study become a basis for the actual investment decision but also alleviate the decision-maker from the direct responsibility for judging technical or marketing merits.

Using Worksheet #4: Exploring the Rewards

Entrepreneurs generally have a keen ability to simplify the issues in front of them. They can instinctively see why something has benefit. They understand reward.

Reward must exist at all levels. Think about the ex-secretary who started the shared office concept. She started by packaging a group of rewards or

WORKSHEET #4
EXPLORING THE REWARDS

1. REASONS THE CLIENT WILL BE HAPPY

Reward perception: ______________________________

____

____

Means to increase: ______________________________

____

____

2. REASONS EMPLOYEES WILL BE HAPPY

Reward perception: ______________________________

____

____

Means to increase: ______________________________

____

____

3. REASONS MANAGEMENT WILL BE HAPPY

Reward perception: ______________________________

____

____

Means to increase: ______________________________

____

____

4. REASONS INVESTORS WILL BE HAPPY

Reward perception: ______________________________

____

____

Means to increase: ______________________________

____

____

5. WHO ELSE GETS REWARDS AND WHAT ARE THOSE REWARDS?

____

____

____

____

____

____

____

benefits that she knew appealed to all independent businesspeople. She identified the financial savings reward of efficiently using equipment like a photocopier, word processor, and receptionist phone system. Statistically, she determined potential profit levels with the single assumption of an average rent figure. From her profits, she earmarked a portion to apply to her financial backers. With a winning personality and a simple summary message, she showed how everybody would win if she went into business.

The prompts in Worksheet #4 are very general and provided only as a guideline. Add specific questions as they apply to your venture and search for all the potential rewards that will be derived. Don't forget the reward that you will employ people and create productivity. That may lead you to government funding sources that support job creation. Or if you can find enough rewards for your potential customer base, you may even convince them to become your financial backers.

d. PUTTING IT TOGETHER

Novice business planners face two basic uncertainties when they take on the challenge of preparing their plan. First, they are not sure of what should be in a plan. Second, they tend to feel uncomfortable about developing the proper format and style of presentation.

These issues are dealt with in the remainder of this book. Each of the following six chapters covers one of the six modules you need to develop to complete your business plan. Worksheets are included in each section to help you isolate the information you need.

As you enter this phase, keep in mind that the content of your plan must eliminate or minimize uncertainty. A good plan will answer all the "W" questions: who, what, where, when, and why. It will also premeditate some of the negative arguments readers of the plan may present.

At this point, you have completed the first four worksheets and you are ready to put the product, marketing, and financial teams into motion. I recommend that the first meeting of team members include all participants from the three planning teams. As the project leader, you can use the four worksheets to clearly summarize the planning calendar and provide suitable background information.

First, explain the parameters of the exercise. Briefly describe your target audience based on the data from Worksheet #1. Set a target date for the three teams to complete their first drafts. Review your team worksheets with a brief explanation of your rationale for the composition of each group. Clearly state your expectations for each team so that individuals and teams know not only what their tasks are but the grander picture of how it all fits together. Invite and field all questions related to the process. Request teams to meet individually and prepare their own agendas to achieve goals. Make sure that every team is aware of its deadlines and has the resources available to complete the job.

e. YOUR CORPORATE STATEMENTS

There are two specific corporate statements that you might wish to introduce at this initial meeting of teams. These can be predefined by you or you might invite the input of your teams. These statements are commonly known as the identity statement and the mission statement.

I suggest that in the interests of expediting the process, you submit your own drafts for discussion by the team and explore ways to collectively improve on them. Both are always open to revision but form a good starting point for all involved.

The completion of identity and mission statements with input from the groups forms an ideal point to launch the module teams on their courses of action. With the mission defined, you can all start toward a common goal.

1. The identity statement

Your identity statement is a single sentence that will accurately describe the essence of your company during the next year. Compare the following descriptions to determine the most effective way to introduce your business.

- Bionic Bicycles makes multi-speed cycles and has sales outlets in 23 states.

  OR

- Bionic Bicycles features their revolutionary transbar pedal mount on six production model 5/10/15-speed mountain bikes and expect to double distribution across the United States by the end of this year.

In the first case, you learn that Bionic makes bikes for half the American market. In the second, you find that the company is working toward full national distribution of a product line aimed at a specific niche of the bicycle market and apparently features a unique design element that sets it apart from its competition. Not only does the second statement tell more about Bionic's business but it establishes an element of curiosity regarding its technology.

The same principle can be applied to small-scale business aimed at a local market:

- Paul's Plumbing Supplies distributes Australian-made faucets, primarily in the Omaha area.

  OR

- Paul's Plumbing, working from its 12,000 square foot warehouse in Omaha, is the exclusive distributor of brand name plumbing hardware for commercial accounts in Nebraska.

Now, draft an identity statement yourself that best distinguishes your business. Write it down. Once you have a concise description of your company, try it out on your staff and a few outsiders to see if it gets your message across. The statement should be simple enough that it can be readily used by you and your associates to describe your main business in all public literature.

2. The mission statement

"Management by objectives" is an established business concept that helps business leaders focus their energies and control the temptation to wander. These objectives should be summarized in two straightforward, concise sentences that the audience will understand. The first can describe long-term objectives; the second should feature the top priorities of the next year. Following are two examples.

- During the next five years, Bionic intends to become a major force in the North American bicycle market and achieve a 6% market share. We are currently shifting our emphasis from product to market development and will double our marketing budget this year to recruit established dealers and expand consumer awareness.
- Paul's Plumbing intends to expand its representation to a full range of high-end household hardware and establish a direct sales force throughout the Midwest over the next five years. The immediate objective is to enhance our reputation for quality service to local building contractors and negotiate exclusive distribution of a Swedish line of door hardware that complements the Dorf plumbing fixtures.

Now, write down your mission statement. State your primary goal for your business for the next five years and your most immediate target.

Identity statement ______________________________

Mission statement ______________________________

3
THE COMPANY AND ITS PRODUCT

As noted earlier, of the six modules that you will build to develop your business plan, four of them form the foundation of the plan: the Company and its Product (or Service), the Marketing Plan, the Financial Plan, and the Team Profile. These four modules are addressed in this and the next three chapters.

The remaining two modules, Concluding Remarks and the Executive Summary, are summaries and will eventually appear as the introduction and conclusion of your plan after all the operational data are gathered (see chapters 7 and 8).

Your first undertaking is to sort out who you are. Are you a technology, exploration, production, or service company? Do you belong to the primary, secondary, or tertiary sectors of the economy? The challenge is to project an image that lifts you above your competitors without appearing too unconventional. Work with the basics, but always look for ways to make your company stand out.

At this stage, you have some idea of who will see the business plan, who will help you prepare it, and the relevant risks and rewards, and you have just summarized your identity statement and business mission. Now begins the task of accumulating the specific data that will form the body of the report. Worksheets #5, #6, #7, and #8 cover the major points common to most businesses: industry matters, the corporate profile, product issues, and service issues. It is possible that you will observe details about your company that I have not covered but that you think are relevant. Space at the bottom of the worksheets allows for any additions.

While all the topics on these worksheets require your consideration, there is no need to dwell over every blank space if you have trouble responding to a specific area. In some cases, through the process of planning, new information or considerations will emerge that may bring you back to insert comments in these spaces.

Before embarking on completing the next four worksheets, you should consider three general aspects of business planning that are relevant to all enterprises: suitability to outside investment, geography, and new technology.

a. IS YOUR COMPANY SUITED TO OUTSIDE INVESTORS?

Some businesspeople find it almost impossible to raise money outside the immediate family. At this stage, you are well enough versed on company data and market position to make that judgment. To help you make that evaluation, consider the perspective of the investor.

Experienced investors can often decide about an investment in a matter of minutes. They like tangible evidence of customer acceptance, and they want to relate personally to your company's business activity.

Pure service businesses face an uphill battle attracting investor money. Even professionals with solid track records have trouble attracting money to labor-intensive programs. Financiers want to see a set product that can be rolled over many times to create profit, not something with endless time-consuming revisions for each new job. A software product designed for easy installation and general use is a far more appealing investment than a package that requires technicians to spend days customizing it to the needs of a single customer.

If you are going to revolutionize an industry or win over the buying public with a new product, it cannot deviate too far from the norm. Ideally, your product addresses a simple, obvious need, and you can prove both the economics and the advantage to the end user in order to gain interest.

I recall meeting a man 20 years ago who was convinced he could revolutionize door installations. He wanted to install door knobs in the wall next to the door, not in the door itself, providing a big improvement in safety. His immediate target market was new hotel and apartment construction. He had spent $50,000 over three years seeking major funding. While his argument for improved security was convincing, the concept was too far outside the norm to gain acceptability. Patents, 30 years of construction experience, and the zeal of a product champion were not enough. Even though he recognized a market demand for improved security, he had gone too far. Consumers might have allowed him to take the doorknob out of the door, but investors wouldn't.

Investors will always lean toward product-oriented projects more than services. Even if you know that success or failure will depend on service, find a way to incorporate a product element in your business plan. If you want to raise money to start a new house painting service in an area that sorely needs one, recognize your investment problem. You are short on product impact. Find something that can make your product unique. Go to a national building show and secure an exclusive supply of some new paint or an application technique or ladder system that will enhance productivity. You have to find some way to distinguish yourself from the entrepreneur next to you.

b. THE MATTER OF GEOGRAPHY

It would be easier to convince people that your labor costs will be lower if you operate in the sunbelt states and require untrained labor than if you operate in Seattle. If you are a heavy energy user, it may be easier to defend a location in western Canada than in Hawaii. If you require employees with advanced technical training, Boston might make more sense than Boise.

Are you dependent on distant suppliers? Is your business seasonal or vulnerable to weather conditions? Acknowledge your geographic risks and deal with them. While there is no need to overstate the uncertainties, list your deepest concerns and your awareness of the level of business risk.

For businesses remote from major markets, one key issue to resolve is shipping. Be prepared to explain shipping procedures, rates, economic order quantities, breakage concerns, competitive advantages and disadvantages, carrier options and reliability, and payment policies.

Using Worksheet #5: Industry Matters

Many existing businesses fail and new businesses never prosper because their leaders do not understand the industry they are in. A classic case was the demise of rail companies that did not recognize that their future should not be tied to metal tracks three feet apart. They were in the transportation business, but they failed, in the first half of the twentieth century, to complement their locomotive base with automobiles, trucks, and airplanes.

WORKSHEET #5
INDUSTRY MATTERS

Industry description: ______________________________

____

____

____

Will you operate locally? __________ regionally? __________ nationally? __________

What are the leading edge companies in the industry? ______________________________

____

____

Reasons for their success? ______________________________

____

____

Stable companies in industry? ______________________________

____

____

Historic highlights of industry? ______________________________

____

____

Key industry data that make you optimistic about the future: ______________________________

____

____

____

____

How does the industry perceive your company? ______________________________

____

____

____

____

Relative to your immediate competitors, your most distinctive company trait is ______________________________

____

____

____

____

____

____

More recently, segments of the computer business have lost their way. In the process of selling computer "magic" in the 1960s, they sold the ability to eliminate human error, often suggesting that the machine was infallible. It wasn't widely stated that the hardware was only as good as the programs that ran it. Most computer companies that emphasized hardware fell victim to the need for quality programs that would make the machines efficient.

In the next phase, the smart people recognized that the key to their industry was the ability to process repetitive information quickly and accurately. The vital business-customer links were at the input and output levels. Companies that created exotic software but failed to edit input precisely and anticipate data entry errors missed the mark. Even today, poor communication between technicians and business managers leads to unsatisfactory output reports that cloud rather than clarify the issues.

The winning companies know that they are electronic accountants, secretaries, or engineers and identify with the responsibilities of assuming those roles. The system output has to meet the accuracy standards set by *people* and deal both with the norm and the exceptions.

During the industry shakeout of the mid-1970s, a few wise men and women started to recognize that being in the office service business meant you were in the people business. Human nature is adverse to change and the computer was changing everything in a cold, misunderstood, and impersonal way. New businesses responded to the problem with the next stage of software and a catch phrase that caught the imagination of the business world: "user friendly." Engineers made smaller black boxes and programmers responded with a new sensitivity to customers. Those who identified specifically with computer power and capacity rather than market needs died quickly.

Ironically, in the 1990s, raw computer power has made a comeback. Demands of the Internet, desktop publishing, and computer games have hardware salespeople bragging about speed and capacity. Rather than provide a niche product, they emphasize a configuration that allows you to "have it all."

In defining the bounds of your industry, remember that they are set more by the mood of the marketplace than by current product specification. We live in a market-driven world. Reflect upon the people you deal with. What are their motivations for being your customers — and what are their expectations? The answers will tell you what business you are in.

Gather timely background data on the business. Your written document must reflect your personal understanding of the industry and project some sense of worldliness — and a broad perspective. References to trends in other markets, quotations on the evolution of the industry, and hints that you are in touch with the world around you will help develop a good impression. It is no sin to adopt good ideas used by similar companies in other markets. Read national trade magazines to reinforce what you know about the local industry. If your business is new to your community but has been successful elsewhere, draw on these examples to illustrate market acceptance.

Completing this worksheet may require a trip to the local library or industry association. If you function within a specific niche of a larger industry, try to concentrate data in areas that relate to your company. Don't get your technology confused with your business. The company that built the world's first tourist submarines soon recognized that it was not in the submarine business as much as it was in the tourist business. You must think of your industry primarily in terms of your marketplace.

While researching your industry, make copies of any authoritative articles that affirm your corporate mission statement or your specific niche.

Using Worksheet #6: General Corporate Profile

This worksheet is an extension of Worksheet #5 in that you are still relating the company to its industry and economic environment. The key difference in how the data are used will come at the point of writing your plan. The data in Worksheet #5 will provide an overview of the industry, while in this worksheet, you will confirm the human and tangible assets that you have available to function in that setting. Finally, you will summarize that the general economic climate is suitable to this business venture proceeding.

On this worksheet provide the legal business name and date established, note the basic qualifications of the founders to form the business (e.g., experience base, education), list the current founders and their planned management relationship, and summarize the company's most tangible current assets.

Position your company in the scheme of things. How many vital suppliers do you have? How many customers do you have? What geographical segment and market niche do you operate in?

Describe your operational setting, current corporate staffing, and intangible factors that may influence the goodwill evaluation of the company.

WORKSHEET #6

GENERAL CORPORATE PROFILE

Name of company: ______________________________

Address of head office: ______________________________

____

Corporate legal counsel: ______________________________

Corporate bankers: ______________________________

Corporate auditors: ______________________________

Names of founders: ______________________________

____

Founders' current relationship to company: ______________________________

____

Major equipment and inventory assets: ______________________________

____

Real estate: ______________________________

Key suppliers: How many? ______________ Do you import? ______________

Are supply prices stable? ______________________________

Names of brand name suppliers: ______________________________

____

____

Key customers: How many? ______________ Do you export? ______________

Does currency fluctuation affect business? ______________________________

Names of major customers: ______________________________

____

____

Describe marketplace: ______________________________

____

____

Describe operational setting: ______________________________

____

____

Key intangible assets to support goodwill evaluation: ______________________________

____

____

____

____

Goodwill is the term used to recognize the value that a company has established through its existence and is a very important concept for all companies intent on raising money. Goodwill arises from corporate reputation, product reputation, or human reputation. Once you determine the actual market value of your tangible assets and separate that from the valuation of the company as an ongoing concern, you have isolated the goodwill factor. The quality of your business plan helps establish the value of your goodwill, and justifying your goodwill component is critical to reconciling investors to the investment cost.

Remember that at this stage you are summarizing basic information that you will consider putting in your plan. It is possible that you will decide not to name customers or average sales figures in your final document to protect confidentiality. At this stage you are only gathering data that can be edited later.

Using Worksheets #7 and #8: Product and Service Issues

You've probably had the experience of eating in a restaurant with good food but lousy service or vice versa. In a competitive environment, quality in one area and incompetence in the other makes success unlikely.

Most companies must pay attention to both the product element and the service element of their enterprise. To many, this seems a major undertaking. But in this day and age, how can a producer/distributor of home fireplaces fail to be open to the public on weekends? Why does a kitchen cabinetmaker buy expensive space at a major home show and then fail to follow up on inquiries? Or how can another cabinetmaker meet a prospective client without material samples or photo documentation of the work? All these cases show a product/service imbalance emerging at the marketing stage.

Astute investors are far more concerned about evaluating how a market will emerge for the given product. They want to know if the business planner has considered the input of the marketplace in designing the product or refining the service. They want to know that the blend of product and service will together fulfill a demand in the marketplace.

Business opportunity will always exist in fields that are infamous for failing to meet the service or product expectations of the end user. This has long been one of the major reasons why ambitious groups of immigrants have come to North America from Asia and Europe and virtually taken over

WORKSHEET #7
PRODUCT ISSUES

In our business, we purchase:

(a) finished products
(b) components
(c) raw materials

We consider our main vulnerability to be:

Pricing of ____________________
Reason: ____________________
Supply of ____________________
Reason: ____________________
Quality of ____________________
Reason: ____________________
Durability of ____________________
Reason: ____________________
Other: ____________________
Reason: ____________________

We have completed a competitive product analysis. Yes ________ No ________

Our main competitive advantages are ____________________

____

____

Our competitive problems are ____________________

____

____

We have interviewed end users of our product and their basic impressions are that ____________________

____

____

____

If we could change one thing in the product component of our business, it would be ____________________

____

____

____

____

____

____

____

WORKSHEET #8
SERVICE ISSUES

In our business service is:

(a) everything
(b) related to product supply
(c) tied to installation and maintenance
(d) a user of products as tools

We consider our main service vulnerability to be:

Cost of ______________________________
Reason: ______________________________
Supply of ______________________________
Reason: ______________________________
Quality of ______________________________
Reason: ______________________________
Training of ______________________________
Reason: ______________________________
Other: ______________________________
Reason: ______________________________

We have completed a competitive service analysis. Yes __________ No __________

Our main competitive advantages are ______________________________

____

____

Our competitive problems are ______________________________

____

____

We have interviewed end users of our service and their basic impressions are that ______________

____

____

____

If we could change one thing in the service component of our business, it would be ______________

____

____

____

____

____

____

service-oriented businesses where the current standards or costs were vulnerable to assertive competition.

Product and service analysis can actually alter your business strategy. As you fill out Worksheets #7 and #8, consider your vulnerability to people, component sources, material and labor costs, import duties, shipping costs, shifts in market taste, competitor pricing, product features, and ongoing service needs. Also explore the adaptability of your product and service components to expand your market penetration.

One aluminum window company I recently interviewed showed me a complete product evaluation — of their product compared to eight competitive products sold in the same marketplace. They were able to illustrate why they had modified their original design to introduce new features and they compared insulation performance, durability, functionality, esthetics, and pricing data to the competition. As a marketing tool, this analysis was extremely useful. The chart would also make impressive reading in a business plan. More impressive, however, was that the company product analysis was complete and concisely presented. They knew where they stood and they were confident in their product. They had also identified the key service concerns of their main customer groups and they developed order fulfillment methods, credit application procedures, and measurement and delivery services to meet customer desires. They set service policies that restricted their involvement outside their field of expertise but provided advice on related suppliers who might complement their efforts.

c. PRODUCTS AND THE INTERNET

The Internet explosion has resulted in a broad interest by businesspeople. "How can I get my product on the Net?" many ask. It would be wrong to downplay the potential of this new phenomenon, but caution is in order.

I liken this stampede to other historic misadventures. Certainly a few people got rich chasing gold to California, the Caribou, or the Klondike — and a small percentage will garner wealth in the rush to cyberspace. However, like in most mass movements to a gold field, the profit will come from facilitating the process, not clawing the mother lode. (See chapter 10 for further discussion of technology.)

4
THE MARKETING PLAN

It is far more than a semantics problem when entrepreneurs and managers interchange the terms "business plan" and "marketing plan." While we live in a market-driven economy where customer sensitivity is vital to success, marketing issues remain but one element of the overall business plan. Granted, they are often the most critical element and for this reason, they should be allotted appropriate emphasis.

Many market-driven business situations prescribe that a detailed marketing plan is required, separate from the business planning document. In some cases, the conclusions and objectives of the marketing plan will truly dictate the priorities of the business plan and will become a given around which the business plan evolves. In other cases, financial constraints or a rigid product definition will dictate that the marketing plan respond more to corporate limitations than to marketplace issues. In this case, the detailed marketing plan may be developed parallel to the overall business strategy and a condensed version of the marketing plan will be incorporated into the business plan.

It seems imminently sensible that a companion volume to this guide should focus on the detailed development of a successful marketing plan, especially in cases where the plan must respond to new and growing markets. However, the discussion in this book is confined to a summary description of the marketing strategy as it applies to the overall business.

Ideally, your product or service is market driven and designed to meet a documented demand in the marketplace. However, market planning usually starts with a given product or service specification already in place. This does not imply that the specification is rigid. In fact, a key part of the role of marketing is to constantly measure that specification against the moods of the marketplace and recommend change as required.

a. A MARKET STUDY

Before anything else, you must prove that your product or service provides viable user benefits to a sizable consumer group. Translated into economic terms, you must verify that customers find enough merit in your product offering to establish a demand — desire plus the ability to pay. Normally this means written proof that customers will buy your product. You do this by conducting a market study.

There are a few ways to get your study done. The most expensive way is to hire a professional market research group. For $5,000 to $100,000 the experts will design a questionnaire, conduct in-depth interviews, explore subconscious reactions, and appraise the quality of consumer input. They will deliver a thick market study and it will say what you told them you wanted to hear. It will help the project get off the ground.

Personally, I think nine out of ten entrepreneurs can avoid the expense of this route by using one of the following three methods:

(a) Set your budget and interview independent consultants to see what they will provide in the way of a marketing study for that fixed price. There are a lot of hungry consultants with time on their hands and you may be surprised what a shopping trip like this will yield.

(b) Enlist the aid of the local university. My submarine-building friend at Sub Aquatics International was most successful in working with a senior student group to create a detailed, useful study related to consumer response to a Caribbean underwater voyage. With the endorsement of the class professor, this entrepreneur worked with a small group of enthusiastic marketing students to design a questionnaire, qualify testing and interview procedures, and provide any support they required to complete the project. Three months later, he paid a modest stipend to support the expansion of the college-business interaction program and received a report that proved very valuable in his fund-raising efforts.

(c) Written testimonials from qualified customers with buying power and the right credentials can replace a full market study in some cases. This is useful particularly where commercial product feasibility is established by estimating the payback period. For example, if a customer testifies that by purchasing your cost-saving device for $5,000, he or she will cut costs by $400 per month, that customer verifies your product's economic viability. A single letter from a respected customer can give your potential investor the most important fact he or she could ever hope to glean from a market study: an acknowledged cost-benefit relationship.

The key goal of all of these methods is to identify the true advantages that users relate to your product. Once the benefit is identified, its value to the user must be established to ensure that your pricing policy will work. Even if 90% of tourists would like to see the coral reefs of Barbados, with a $3-million submarine, you won't make any money if you charge only $4 per hour.

The most common user benefit to review is direct financial savings. For example, a good window sales representative will always carry a copy of an energy report that illustrates the direct fuel cost reductions to be gained by installing double-glazed windows.

Economic benefits can be direct or indirect and are especially relevant if you target commercial users. Products that help reduce operating costs for a business must obviously save more than they cost. Such benefit analysis calls for a precise comparison of costs before and after inclusion of your product or service in the potential customer's operation.

Worksheet #9 is aimed at assisting you to distinguish user benefits and their associated value.

Using Worksheet #9: User Benefits and Their Value

America's fast-growing golf industry provides a good example of entrepreneurial problems and creativity to establish user benefit. Every January, the annual Professional Golf Association Merchandise Mart in Orlando unveils a new selection of products. Directly or indirectly, benefit for golfers must be translated into a lower golfing score — or so you would think. One astute observer at this show pointed out that only about a third of the displays at this show were concerned with the game of golf and the pursuit of lower scores. Two-thirds of the booths catered to the social peripherals of golf.

WORKSHEET #9
USER BENEFITS AND THEIR VALUE

We feel that the prime user benefits attached to our product/service are ______________________________

____

____

To project these benefits we use the following techniques: ______________________________

____

____

____

____

User response indicates that they rate benefits as follows: ______________________________

____

____

____

Benefits we feel they underrate are ______________________________

____

____

____

To overcome this we have ______________________________

____

____

____

Our research indicates that the user values our benefits to justify pricing as follows: ______________________________

____

____

____

Our support documentation to justify these deductions includes: ______________________________

____

____

____

User expectations that we do not currently meet include: ______________________________

____

____

____

User demand for features we plan to consider in the future include: ______________________________

____

____

____

Peering over acres of displays and 1,000 booths, he concluded that golf was obviously a very social game.

For the observer, this meant that manufacturers of pink putters, porcelain drivers, and cashmere sweaters were not out to prove user benefit in the form of lower scores, but more in the rewards associated with feeling stylish or flamboyant. In other words, manufacturers were meeting psychological needs. The good marketers knew they were in the personal grooming business, not the golf business. The observer did not explore this product motivation any further but turned, instead, to a five-foot long pendulum putter held by senior professional golfer Charles Owens.

"Can you imagine the effort required to prove user benefit from that thing? I guess anything is possible," he said.

The observer had missed one key point. The strange putter he questioned was being made and sold under license by a company with a wider product range. The originator had recognized the user-benefit dilemma early. He would waste a lot of time trying to convince non-golfing investors of his product potential. He went directly to experienced marketers who knew the pulse of the pro shop and were themselves walking data banks of consumer demands. Golfers would putt with a monkey wrench if it would help the ball reach the hole.

This story shows that there is always a way to overcome obstruction. But in some instances, such as the case of an unorthodox putter, you will save time and frustration by relating solely to people who know your marketplace.

Worksheet #9 is a summary statement sheet. More than any other worksheet in this chapter, it requires ongoing backup documentation to support the statements you make. Letters, statistical surveys, interview documentation, testimonial references — the more the better.

b. THE MARKETING PLAN PROCEDURE

There are four steps in the marketing plan procedure: defining the market, summarizing objectives and strategy, preparing your marketing game plan, and monitoring reaction and sales productivity. Again, you can use the accompanying worksheets to help gather data valuable to your marketing plan. The objective is to set down data you will need when you are ready to present your business plan.

1. Define the market

How do you get a handle on your potential market? Most entrepreneurs have some idea of market scope but have trouble expressing themselves. Consider these basics.

If your business operates out of a fixed location that requires direct customer interaction, a mall for example, your market scope is limited geographically. The same applies to national sales distribution of expensive lawn furniture where your market profile centers on homeowners with above-average disposable income who enjoy living in a mild climate.

Market segmentation and/or niche market definition are extremely important to start-up businesses with limited budgets. There is no faster way in business to waste money than to aim at the wrong target customer. This is the primary reason people try to expand their vision by reading books on demography. Worksheet #10 is designed to help you narrow down satisfactory market priorities, but, before you start, you must deal with three key aspects of market definition.

(a) Estimate its size and profile

Staggering amounts of written documentation from the telephone book to library shelves full of market data will help you estimate the size and profile of the market. A clear statement describing your market segment and its growth trends is an important first step.

DEMOGRAPHICS: CUTTING TO THE CHASE

Demographics refers to the characteristics of population segments. In business, its focus is fixed on the study of consumer markets. Taken at their worst, essays on human traits can end up being nothing more than a stereotyping of individuals into a common group because of age, sex, education, location, or some other social indicator. At best, the interpretation of demographic data is about as accurate as weather forecasting. Demographers may generalize about the relevance of education to success, but they cannot explain why 50% of North American millionaires never finished college. Nor can they provide the slightest clue as to why more than half the CEOs and U.S. senators and presidents graduated in the bottom half of their class. Still, books on demographics rule the bestseller lists as these words are written.

In an age when political correctness can reclassify normal people into racists, sexists, fascists, or the latest "*ist* of the month," an insatiable public has embraced demography as a risk-free subject for both earnest dialogue and cocktail-hour drivel. With that in mind, here are some basic considerations for the business planner.

Demographics does not explain two-thirds of everything, no matter what David Foot (author of *Boom, Bust & Echo*) claims. His former student Derek Holt, now an economist with the Royal Bank of Canada, recently countered such claims.

"Demographics is not the road to riches for someone developing a business plan or investment strategy," Holt stated. Countering Foot's thesis that birth rate trends over the past 50 years are the critical social change in our free enterprise society, Holt and other traditionalists in the world of economics see central banks and inflation control as far more relevant to tomorrow's business conditions. Both sides provide food for thought, but neither identifies the fundamental problem with demographics as a source of great knowledge.

In business, the art of planning is aimed at filling an economic desire; it is an issue of supply and demand. Demographics deals solely with demand as it zones in on consumer habits as they relate to human traits. Age is the trait in the spotlight these days. A word of warning: using age patterns to speculate on demand trends without being equally respectful to factors that can impact product development or global trade can spell economic ruin for the poor planner.

That said, many small businesses that rely on local or regional buying power have good reason to grasp the demographic message. Most of this decade's early retirees were born during the Great Depression or World War II. A blend of voluntary retirees and victims of corporate merger, tough-love management, and the golden handshake are now creating a healthy mob of well-off people who plan to live as comfortably as possible for at least two decades.

The phenomenon of the post-war baby boom and the dramatic swings in birth rates between the 1950s and the 1970s has led to a very different economic profile for people in different age brackets. On average, kids born in the 1950s had three siblings and half a television set. Compared to the past two decades, life was good.

In a democracy, when this group reached voting age, they became all powerful. By then they had lived through the layered experience of the 1960s and were pairing off, while embracing the merits of the pill. Women were spreading their wings, fully unaware that a man's world wasn't all it was cracked up to be. Both sexes managed to earn euphemisms such as "the Me Generation" along the way, and that was not good news for the lesser group (in number if nothing else) trailing behind. Babies of the late 1960s would earn the classification "Generation X" and are apparently destined to be seen as lost souls forever — or in many cases until their well-to-do parents die.

Arguably, demographics can be used to predict trends as aging boomers hang up their skis to play golf and occasionally spoil their grandchildren. The literature is worth reading to grasp the relevance to both your own business and geographic location. Is an onslaught of boomer retirees likely to move your way, ready to acquire new creature comforts that your business provides? Will immigrants take their place?

In the business world, demographics is really all about who has the discretionary income and what we expect to be tomorrow's discretion.

(b) Estimate the projected economic climate

Predicting trends in business climate can be tough. Interest rate trends, unemployment rates, local housing starts, and a general assessment of the mood of the marketplace probably will serve you just as well as relying on some national economic guru to forecast the future national business climate. About half the economists will be partially right on the mix of fiscal trends and conditions (e.g., unemployment, inflation, interest rates, currency relationships) that will prevail in the next two to five years. The other half will be wrong. On top of this uncertainty, you must evaluate your ability to adapt to trend reversals and unforeseeable factors. Nobody knows what the next international disaster will be. Talk to anybody who was locked into prime-plus floating mortgages in the early 1980s when interest rates doubled with the speed of light. It was not a good time.

(c) Estimate the number of competitors

Estimating your competitors is the Achilles heel of market planning. Just about everybody underestimates the level of competition they will face. If you look at any major urban center that has flourished in the past 20 years and briefly review the fluctuation of vacancy rates in office towers, you will see how even the best underestimate competition. Developers look at the status quo, assess a growing demand for space, and start building. Each, caught up in his or her own vision, ignores the fact that six others have the same idea.

Market studies are usually done in confidence, and you must recognize the possibility that others are making similar plans to yours at the same time. New competition will emerge as you do. Unless you offer a rare, patent-protected product to a captive audience, the free enterprise system will guarantee you a rival.

Worksheets #10, #11, and #12 are designed to help with your individual situation while addressing these key aspects of market definition. Worksheet #10 is a summary sheet aimed at issues you may expand on in your final written report. It will also help you to refine your overall marketing strategy. The entrepreneur who studies, understands, and respects his or her competition is the one most often supported by professional investors.

Using Worksheet #10: Segmenting the Market

Let's agree that there are three general buyer's markets in North America: consumer, commercial, and government. Very few businesses target all three as viable. Although unusual surprise markets can emerge for a product (people using Preparation H for facials is my favorite), most producers have some sense of their customer group traits. They may be less attuned to the characteristics of the market itself.

Consider the following points as you fill in Worksheet #10:

(a) *Market scope:* Are there geographic limitations on your marketing program? Can you efficiently develop national representation? If so, and if you are doing business in Canada, for example, is it feasible to cross the border and do business in the United States? Do franchise agreements or distribution constraints restrict you geographically? Does the customer have to be attracted to a single showroom site to do business or can you go to him or her? Can alternate promotion campaigns broaden your market? Does it lend itself to television, telephone, or direct mail merchandising?

WORKSHEET #10

SEGMENTING THE MARKET

Our initial geographical market boundaries are ______________________________

____

Our primary customer profile is estimated to include potential buyers with the lead target markets located

____

We have/will run test markets in ______________________________
aiming to achieve a ____________% acceptance rate of our product.
The traits that best describe our target customer profile include: ______________________________

____

____

____

To gather market information, our major sources were ______________________________

____

____

____

The customer profile traits that are most important to us when we set out to prove the user benefit of our product include: ______________________________

____

____

____

The best "expert" quotation we have found to support our perception of market opportunity is__________

____

____

____

The most important statistical data we have gathered originated______________________________

____

____

____

A summary of that data is attached. (Gather support data that may be incorporated in a written report.)

____

____

____

____

____

____

(b) *Trends in market size:* Is the market growing or shrinking? Can statistical studies provide profile data on age, income, education, sex, and other distinguishing measures? Libraries and city halls house endless studies related to metropolitan statistical areas, building trends, traffic counts, regional economic plans, and projected job growth. Don't overlook secondary sources related to regional consumer traits as well. For example, an analyst may see a trend to more housing starts per capita in the east than the west. If you are in the dishwasher business, that may be enough to lure you to the east. If you are in the window or drapery business, your decision is missing key information. Further statistical research would tell you that there are 25 windows per house in the west but only 14 in the east.

(c) *Timely data sources:* One of the problems with statistical data sources in a dynamic economy is their current relevance. I recommend developing at least one summary chart of your marketplace that uses the most current information possible. Local newspapers, telephone yellow page listings, and regional real estate boards can provide input to project development patterns in the consumer and commercial markets.

National and regional trade shows also yield current data on developing markets. There are some regions that traditionally have led the way in consumer trends, California being the pacesetter in many areas. In Canada, I know one eastern distributor who travels annually to the west to get a sense of what will be "hot" the following year. The ability to portray the future with existing references can serve you well.

(d) *Review accepted futuristic readings:* It never hurts to quote a visionary source like *Megatrends, Future Shock, Entrepreneur Magazine* or *Inc.* to reinforce your market conclusions. This research not only can provide enlightening data on your particular field but can demonstrate your ability to stay in tune with market changes. Specific trade journals also tend to be more timely than government statistical reports.

Using Worksheet #11: Knowing the Competition

Here the subject is marketplace competition as distinct from product competition. For example, if you are vying for the discretionary leisure time of consumers, the market competition goes well beyond competitors offering attractions similar to yours. Once you have developed a clear picture of your

WORKSHEET #11

KNOWING THE COMPETITION

a. DIRECT COMPETITION

The best marketers who provide similar products in our marketplace are ______________________

____

____

Estimated market share for each of our major competitors is ______________________

____

____

Targets to win over market share include: ______________________

____

____

Advantages and disadvantages of our location relative to competitive sites include: ______________________

____

____

A consumer awareness survey of key industry competitors indicates ______________________

____

____

____

Attached is a summary of our pricing, warranty policy, promotional incentives, distribution network, and other factors as compared to key competitors. Our main competitive edge is

____

____

____

b. INDIRECT COMPETITION

Our indirect competition comes from ______________________

____

We expect this to grow/decline for the following reasons: ______________________

____

____

c. UNKNOWN COMPETITION

Unknown competition is of concern to us for the following reasons: ______________________

____

____

____

We anticipate the following competitive trend: ______________________

____

____

product and its potential customer group, a full analysis of competing forces is required. As previously stated, competitive analysis is where many business planners fall down. Think of competition as originating from three different sources: direct, indirect, and unknown.

Fred Adler, a highly regarded American venture capitalist, cites lack of details on competition, direct and indirect, as among the red flags that worry him most in business plans. He also states that his initial 10-minute scan of a business plan is largely to evaluate the tone and honesty of the plan. Plans that knock the competition bother him. These points are worth keeping in mind.

Direct competition is the easiest to address. Direct competitors are best described as those seeking the same customer base with essentially the same product group. In the previous module, the competitive product analysis helped identify the major rival product/service component. Now a summary to distinguish your product and marketing philosophy would be helpful. Competitive analysis should not stop at the product specification and price comparison. You must evaluate all elements.

How do warranties and installation policies compare? What is the difference in promotion techniques? Do all the competitors sell and distribute the same way? Is there a particular company to model yourself after? Don't be afraid to mimic success or study and modify it for more success. After all, the Japanese created the most dynamic economy of the 1980s after analyzing and copying the competition.

You might also want to study a similar business outside your own market. Many successful businesses tie their roots to adopting a full corporate marketing philosophy that was successful in one competitive market and simply shifting to a new market. Some are called business clones; others are called franchises. In fact, corporate cloning has many of the advantages of franchising without the royalty fees.

Businesses operating at the local or regional level have a real opportunity in this area. Many good ideas have been carried from town to town or country to country with success. In some cases, you may have to pay for detailed information, recipes, operations manuals, etc., but you will likely find that by including a successful formula, endorsed and proven by its originator, you reduce the perceived risk of your venture.

Indirect competition deals with alternate products/services going after the same discretionary dollars. If you invest in a golf driving range, the bowling alley two blocks away is indirect competition. If you plan to make and sell hot tubs in a suburban area, you must assess the other home service suppliers who are competing for the same dollars.

Virtually every consumer or business has limited funding and must make choices on what to buy today and what to postpone or eliminate from the budget. This can be a very subtle area of analysis and is particularly critical in retailing and consumer-oriented services.

A butcher might consider other meat suppliers as direct competition but ignore the neighborhood fish store. If the latter has better parking, friendlier service, a quality product, and attractive pricing, it can substantially affect the butcher's business.

Unknown competition is a subject few business planners write about. How can you discuss the unknown? The key is anticipation.

As your success grows or the potential of your business becomes more obvious, other entrepreneurs will consider the same market. Maybe they will quietly commit to leased space or capital equipment purchases oblivious of your existence. Maybe they will be aggressive, ambitious, or stupid and intend to compete head on and outlast you to win a market demand that can support only one business.

Dealing with unknown competition boils down to astute anticipation of marketplace dynamics. Technology bursts like facsimile machines, cellular telephones, and computer games open small opportunity windows for short periods. The competitive situation changes daily.

Although the factor of unknown competition may seem impossible to deal with in your business plan, it is not. Consider the case of the astute home flooring contractor who secured regional rights to a European line of hardwood flooring materials. "After years in the carpeting business, I have concluded that this segment of the floor covering trade will not be a part of our new business. We will specialize in hardwood. Ironically, we anticipate that one trend in carpeting will greatly enhance our new business. The large influx of oriental area carpets into our community is the result of immigrants bringing assets from their homeland. While this phenomenon may capture a share of the carpet business, it will do nothing but enhance the demand for hardwood. In five years, we expect that many in today's carpet market will blame this unknown competitor for their demise, but we will point to it as a contributor to our success."

This single paragraph, complete with its subjective judgments, may seem superfluous. However, to the keen-eyed investor, it is indicative of an entrepreneur capable of anticipating trends in the marketplace.

There are ways to reduce the unknowns and eliminate risks as you develop competitive knowledge. This is a difficult area to write about in the business plan, but a simple paragraph that demonstrates your foresight regarding unknown competition will impress your readers. Demonstrate the intent to grow at a pace suited to achieving realistic market penetration and discouraging market entry from newcomers.

Using Worksheet #12: The Economic Climate

Don't clutter your report with a load of mildly relevant economic data. If you are supplying bathroom fixtures to new home construction sites, a comment on interest rates and their affect on housing starts is very important, but a dissertation on the relationship of the U.S. dollar to the Japanese yen is going too far.

In most reports, this section should be kept short. As a small business operator, you are aiming to demonstrate two things in this section of your business plan:

(a) you are reasonably aware that the national economy exists and that you are not lost in your own small world; and,

(b) you recognize that economic factors, over which you have no control, can affect you, and your planning takes into account this vulnerability.

Local issues are often more important than national ones. Oil price trends are more important to Texas or Alberta than national employment rates. Environmental issues like acid rain, toxic waste, or oil spills can take precedence over economic merit in certain instances and should be addressed as a part of this section if relevant.

The importance of socio-economic factors varies dramatically among businesses, so it is important not to downplay this section. Dramatic international incidents can result in numerous business opportunities, and if you are astute enough to foresee a major occurrence it can do little harm to include a brief comment in this section. For example, if a packaged tour promoter focused on Alaska and Caribbean cruises rather than the Mediterranean in the mid-1980s because he or she anticipated the possibility of a ship hijacking, hindsight would prove the promoter wise. A brief comment in the business plan describing this rationale would likely have no negative affect on the impression the plan left even if a hijacking had not occurred.

WORKSHEET #12
THE ECONOMIC CLIMATE

The major national economic factors that help determine our future business climate include:

The major regional economic factors that help determine our future business climate include:

The biggest concern we have about economic conditions is

The most encouraging factor related to the current economic state is

Increased inflation will affect us as follows:

Increased interest rates will affect us as follows:

Unemployment rates affect us as follows:

Currency exchange rates affect us as follows:

A recent "expert" quotation on the economy that supports our endeavor is

Remote statistical economic data can also sometimes serve your plan's effectiveness. The national surge in golf course construction in 1988/89 was not that hard to foresee if you looked at the tremendous growth in golf club purchases in 1986/87. By digging deep enough to reveal some economic relationship that the business plan reader has no knowledge of, you can score valuable points for your program.

2. Summarize marketing objectives and strategy

I am a firm believer in setting challenging business objectives and forming a strategy that makes them attainable. At the same time, I have little patience with goals that are naive and impractical. Most financial analysts will share these biases. Marketing and financial objectives are intertwined to the point that they meet on an income statement line called net revenue. However, the route to that crossroad requires a specific description of the marketing objectives.

You have to make one basic decision that has more to do with your personality than your marketing skills: whether or not you are going to employ a "hidden agenda." Do you want an internal effort and targets that aim higher than your true expectation? Is it useful to generate internal goals separate from those announced publicly? When you sit in a sales meeting six months from now giving a pep talk to your staff, will their market share targets be the same as those written into the business plan?

The decision to use the hidden agenda technique is a very personal one. I am an advocate of it because it is both fun and effective.

The reason the hidden agenda technique must be addressed early in the planning process is to avoid any misinterpretation by staff or external readers. Think of it in terms of distinguishing your marketing objectives from your marketing targets. Targets are set higher than your stated objectives and performance-oriented staff are encouraged to use their personal energies and resources to hit the bull's-eye. While your objectives will be tied directly to budgets and consistent with stated goals in the business plan, targets are set for overachievers, energetic, results-oriented employees who will reap generous rewards for exceeding objectives.

While you are developing your marketing objectives and related strategy, keep in mind the areas where you can establish related targets for internal use. Targets must always refer to the basic objective and are best kept to a simple incentive formula. For example, if you develop an objective of opening a new market and setting up ten new accounts in the next six months, you might increase the staff reward by 20% for all new accounts beyond ten. This tiered incentive provides an added emphasis on meeting your objectives. All additional incentive costs are incurred only after you have achieved objectives. The only factor that you must guard against is employees sacrificing the pursuit of one objective because of incentives attached to another.

It is here where the blend of marketing objectives and related strategy is critical. Use Worksheets #13 and #14 to develop major marketing objectives and set out your strategy statement.

Using Worksheet #13: Setting Marketing Objectives

Concentrate on first-year goals. Don't bother to tell your reader that you plan to become the world leader in your field within five years. This is a matter of objectives, not dreams. Leave it to the strategy summary to deal with the more subtle implications of your goals.

Note that there is an emphasis not only on where you will target your marketing effort but on the protection of your existing market share. Many companies preoccupied with new markets fail to tend to existing business well enough to avoid losing it to a competitor.

Pricing strategy and its effect on the volume of business is a subject that comes up time and again in business planning. Make sure that all references to it through the planning process are consistent in logic.

You should always have a marketing objective aimed at product enhancement; change is a necessary part of growth in this decade. Rare is the company that can boast of being the best because they stayed the same.

One of the easiest ways to support increased sales expectations is to broaden distribution. However, while it might increase sales it will also increase costs. Make sure that your objective can be financially defended.

Promotion objectives should not focus on expenditures with no guaranteed recovery. It is not a positive objective to aim at having the biggest grand opening ever.

Using Worksheet #14: The Marketing Strategy

Your strategy summary must be broader in thinking than the immediate objectives; it is aimed at long-term success. It cannot be tainted by what Theodore Levitt called "marketing myopia." Almost three decades ago, Levitt and his Harvard-based disciples established a clear distinction

WORKSHEET #13
SETTING MARKETING OBJECTIVES

To expand our business we plan to increase market share by______________________________

____

____

We also plan to pursue new markets by ____________________________________

____

____

To protect our existing business we must___________________________________

____

____

Our historic pricing strategy has provided a__________% profit margin and our current objective is to increase/maintain/decrease margins with the expected result to increase/maintain/decrease unit sales volumes. Our goal is to increase total gross profit by_________% solely as a result of this change.

Our objective is to expand distribution by_____________________________________

____

____

To continue the ongoing process of product enhancement we will_______________________

____

____

Promotion goals for the near future include: __________________________________

____

____

We plan to expand our sales effort by______________________________________

____

____

____

The first three steps to achieving these goals are

1. ____

____

2. ____

____

3. ____

____

Our ultimate sales goal for the first year is___________________________________

____

____

WORKSHEET #14

THE MARKETING STRATEGY

Our planned pursuit of increased market share and new markets is based on ________________________

We have revised/not revised our pricing strategy because ________________________

We expect this strategy to be in effect until ________________________

Current distribution objectives are the beginning of a strategy to ________________________

Our long-term product strategy ties to current objectives because ________________________

Our promotion philosophy is ________________________

Tying these strategies to sales goals, we foresee the ability to grow at __________% per annum over the next five years. Critical to this strategy is ________________________ between the marketing and selling functions. Selling concentrates on a company's need to exchange inventory for cash. By contrast, marketing focuses on the needs of the customer. Marketing strategy must respond to information gained from the field and establish a clear understanding within the organization of the expectations of the customer. Regardless of the industry you represent, you must set a marketing strategy that is aimed at client satisfaction.

You can increase market share and open new markets only because you satisfy customers. Distribution strategy must ensure customer convenience and efficient supply of your product. Promotion techniques must recognize what turns customers off as well as what turns them on. Product warranty policy is a response to consumer security needs.

It is important that you develop your statements in this worksheet with the customer perspective in mind. Where possible, try to point out that your decisions have been made based on input from your target customers. As they review your market strategy, readers will tend to assess it from the role of the consumer and expressions of marketplace sensitivity will always serve you well.

3. The marketing game plan

With your immediate objectives set and a customer-responsive strategy articulated, it is time to prepare a summary of how you will execute your program. The best impression to leave in this section is that you know exactly what you are going to do in the next 12 months with your marketing and sales budget. Show that you're on the right track and well in control of the situation.

Some companies attempt to separate sales and marketing responsibilities and budgets where different managers are accountable. In smaller entities, I think this is a mistake. Sales plans are a direct extension of marketing strategy, and the game plan must address the company's need to sell.

Tangible examples of your current status (e.g., price lists, brochures, distributorship literature, user manuals, warranty policies) and a summary of forthcoming expenses (e.g., trade shows, sales kits, sales travel requirements, training agendas, product literature, and sales tool requirements) should be available as supplements to your business plan summary. Consider including a copy of a brief document that outlines how your sales network operates. See Appendix 3 for an example of a corporate sales management document that demonstrates that a game plan is in place.

The game plan shifts the marketing emphasis from customer need to corporate revenue needs. It must illustrate the rationale behind your selling methods and describe the techniques you will employ to let the marketplace know you exist. There are four issues to deal with:

(a) The relationship of sales staffing to product pricing

(b) The ability of the company to generate media interest

(c) The promotion agenda

(d) The intent to go to your customer

(a) The relationship of sales staffing to product pricing

Your sales personnel must have a clear understanding of the nature of your product. We have all heard stories of the successful entrepreneur who invested life savings in a unique gadget and plodded door to door selling it out of a broken-down car. Then one day he was discovered by the international marketers and success followed. Look at this situation closer. A competent distributor had to find the product because the inventor did not pursue the logical distribution channel.

As a general rule, company executives should not be directly involved in the sales effort unless

(a) the sale is critical to corporate survival,

(b) order fulfillment will require substantial capital investment,

(c) the transaction is regarded as a door opener to bigger orders, or

(d) the annual customer sales will exceed $100,000.

The biggest dilemma most companies face is the choice between hiring an internal sales force and recruiting independent agents to represent their interests. Many industries have proponents of both techniques. You should also consider whether your sales representatives will sell your product exclusively or carry it as part of a broader line. The whole issue comes down to dollars and cents for all concerned and that reflects on the price of your product.

You cannot propose to pay somebody $25,000 per year plus a car allowance to drive down a highway selling $40 orders every 50 miles and gain investor respect. The numbers do not make sense. Likewise, it would be imprudent to turn over the sale of a sophisticated energy monitoring system to a towel vendor just because he or she visits every hotel in the state once a year.

At a minimum, you must have one experienced sales representative or manager internally who knows your marketplace and the ground rules of industry distribution. Once you inherit this overhead, don't expand your sales force internally unless it will increase revenue ten times the proposed salary. The mandate of any lead sales person in an organization should be to organize external representation capable of bringing in $1 million per year or add a second internal person only after reaching sales of $40,000 to $50,000 per month.

If your product lists for under $500, the main distribution option is wholesale regional coverage by mass distributors such as magazine rack jobbers who deal in small quantities of numerous products. This still requires an in-house sales manager to coordinate distribution. Packaging, pricing, and mass media promotion strategy are very important.

(b) The ability of the company to generate media interest

If you are planning to open a new carpet cleaning company and you hold a news conference, rent a small room. Few businesses have the sex appeal to draw media attention. Don't underestimate yourself though. With the amount of trade journals and competing media in North America, a little creativity can make a good story out of anything.

If you can't find a media angle yourself, interview publicity agents to assist you. Ask for proposals and budgets after providing an introduction to your company. It will cost nothing until you select your agency. There is nothing that adds an air of credibility like the media acknowledging your existence. This is especially valuable to new technology companies seeking recognition in their industry journals. You may even go as far as sponsoring a freelance writer to develop articles about your company and submit them to receptive periodicals.

(c) The promotion agenda

Explain how you are going to get your company and product known. If your annual budget is $50,000, find a way to stretch it as far as you can and be prepared to defend your plan. A lot of companies waste large sums of money on glossy brochures that don't meet requirements; content is more important than gloss (although sometimes gloss and a smiling face is all it takes), but a broader allocation of promotion budget normally leaves a better impression.

(d) The intent to go to your customer

Make it very clear that you are allowing for the expense and time involved in pursuing your customer. You cannot plan to hang out a shingle and wait for people to knock on your door. You must be close enough to your market that travel cost is feasible to reach it and you must have targets for sales call quotas, sales reporting systems, and customer follow-up procedures.

The same rule applies to finding sales representatives and distributors. National trade shows are ideal places to find representation in different regions. Plan to attend two next year. A second choice when recruiting agents is to bring in a quality national sales manager to help with this single task. Find a respected individual with a non-competing company, one who knows the rep network well. For a $5,000 retainer, this person can make a few telephone calls, open a few doors, and help put together your agent base in a quarter of the time it would take you.

Now use Worksheet #15 to expand your report presentation. This section of the business plan is normally carefully perused. Readers will evaluate how far along you really are as an organization and if you are on the right track. No matter how good your product, you will have to demonstrate a viable sales approach. What you say here will determine how much credibility readers place in your forthcoming sales forecasts.

Using Worksheet #15: The Sales Program

It is vital for a company to develop sales staff compatible with its product image and customer base. Upbeat fast food chains seek personable, energetic teenagers to serve a predominantly under-35 crowd. IBM sought out "All American" boys with a look of good breeding and integrity. Playboy went a long way based on bunny suits and the bodies that filled them.

There are no hard and fast rules and some can be hard to justify on paper. I know one sales manager who assigned accounts according to the age of the buyer. Buyers over 50 got youthful sales representatives who appealed to a sense of paternalism or maternalism. They would open doors with, "I'm new to this territory but I've got a great product to sell and I hope you'll bear with me while I get my feet wet." Young buyers were always approached by male reps in their forties and so on.

You don't need to include all the details, but do go so far as to prepare one of your best sales people to make a sales call on any potential investor. If the rep can sell the product and illustrate your sales program, that will go a long way toward promoting the merits of the company and your business plan.

WORKSHEET #15
THE SALES PROGRAM

Describe the existing/planned sales force including all incentive terms and territorial coverage: ________

Describe planned sales staff growth: ________

Name key sales people with proven track records: ________

Explain projected average order size and order expectations from sales staff: ________

Is product packaging, lot pricing strategy, and promotion consistent with target order size?
Illustrate: ________

Describe how unit product price affects the nature of your sales force. What sales training is required? ________

What will be your three biggest promotion expenditures in the next year? ________

Where do you usually meet your customers? ________

You may find that a brief explanation of your packaging, lot pricing, and sales literature can point out sales aids that are not readily obvious to the untrained. Packaging two flashlight batteries or light bulbs increases unit sales. California Cooler is sold in four-packs rather than six to keep the price below a resistance barrier. Keep sales literature generic and flexible to allow for inserts and sheet replacements so it won't become outdated.

You must demonstrate that your product pricing, territory size, and sales expectations are realistic for your sales staff. If an analyst feels that your sales force will become dissatisfied with commissions and foresees high turnover, you have a problem. Illustrate not only attractive remuneration potential but a road to career growth. (See Appendix 3.)

The dynamics of business in North America make attendance at industry trade shows a must. If you plan to exhibit at a show, try to attend the prior year or talk to vendors who have. Often the location of a booth can be very important to a small company. Know if it is a selling show or a social gathering. Clearly outline the expected costs and expectations from such an endeavor.

4. Monitoring market reaction and sales productivity process

Many business plans forget to include a brief overview of how the company monitors performance and gets feedback from the field.

Hotels and airlines often use guest survey cards to perform this function. My local auto service center calls two weeks after servicing to confirm satisfaction with their work. Good sales managers make random calls into all territories to verify proper servicing of key accounts. I know of one regional marketing vice president in the department store business who reviews every customer complaint personally and frequently contacts customers directly. In his mind, failure to respond to the concerns of established customers is the ultimate marketing sin.

It can be simple and of little cost, but you should establish a means of getting feedback from the end user of your product. At least once a year supplement this by conducting in-depth interviews with a cross section of customers and analyze the results. Think of this as a marketing audit. Odds are it will make you more money and cost less than the financial audit that is a part of standard corporate life.

A sales performance monitoring system is a sign of good management. Throughout your business plan readers will be looking for strengths and weaknesses. Sales performance means more than good customer service. Monitoring systems must also measure productivity. How often do your sales reps make customer contact? Do they prepare call reports for management? Is there an adequate mix of prospecting for new accounts or are sales staff simply servicing their established customers? What is your average sales per active account compared to last year?

Productivity assessment can go beyond the sales team. What is your expected sales per company employee? One Toronto-based computer rental company, Drexis Inc., watched its revenue per employee almost triple in three years and make the grand transition from a break-even company to a profitable one.

Servicing and product installation also require productivity monitoring. In a recent home construction project, I had a first-hand look at the difference between organized and disorganized installation crews. When one company made four different trips with a crew of two and took more than 30 hours of travel time to receive installation revenue of $300, I knew they had a management problem. Later I asked the owner how he monitored his installation crews. His shrug said it all.

5
THE FINANCIAL PLAN

a. PREPARING A FINANCIAL PLAN THAT WILL BE READ

The introduction of simple-to-use spreadsheet programs has eliminated the tedious, time-consuming task of revising budgets and financial forecasts manually. Accurate, detailed pro forma financial statements can now be altered and revisions spit out by computers as fast as needed.

The new problem is overkill. Reams of detailed monthly, quarterly, and annual budgets based on a range of assumptions, growth patterns, and profit margins clutter up standard business plans. What was once noted for its sparseness is now used to "bulk out" skimpy reports.

The novelty of extensive detail has worn thin with business analysts who know how easy it is to generate volumes of financial statements with a spreadsheet program. You will be best served if you feature three or four pages of financial statements which will be judged on the following:

(a) The quality of the assumptions on which they are based

(b) The manner in which they relate to operating financial records and format

(c) The practicality of your program, its time frame, and your cash flow projections

Your financial information should illustrate attractive growth, long-term profits, and equity buildup. Commonly, this takes the form of a five-year forecast, although the reason for this time span is more convention than common sense. Many high-tech businesses, for instance, will either make it big within two years or be a total bust.

Regardless of how conservative you are, readers of your plan will likely discount your numbers because they know that entrepreneurs are optimists who overstate their potential and try to sell their dreams. Therefore, don't be too conservative in your estimates. You are the champion of the cause; if you adopt a role of total objectivity, in spite of your good intentions, it will serve little purpose.

In financial forecasting, you must pay keen attention to both profitability and cash flow and the differences between them. The former is important to accountants who strive to accurately allocate expenses and revenues within a common time frame (monthly or yearly). The latter is more important to investors with cash exposure who assess risk in terms of payback periods and maximum cash requirements to turn around a business. As a result, the format of your financial presentation should provide for disparities between profit and cash flow.

Your financial plan must demonstrate that it is prudent to infuse money into your company to expand profits and/or generate cash on an attractive schedule. In most cases, where new cash is being invested as a part of the business plan, you should emphasize, through reasonable financial detail and support documentation, that you can reach break-even sales volumes and a positive cash flow. Normally, you should be able to show that you plan to achieve this level over a maximum of two years. Once this is done, you can identify the effect of higher sales volumes on fixed overheads and profit margins to illustrate the growing profitability that you will achieve as your business expands.

In this section, I must assume that you have a general understanding of financial statements and their specific role. Businesspeople must understand the following terms:

(a) *Balance sheet:* a point-in-time summary of the depreciated cost of your business assets that equals your business debts plus your net equity position

(b) *Income statement:* a reflection of sales and expense activity over a defined period of time

(c) *Source and use of funds statement or statement of changes in financial position:* a reflection of the actual cash movement within the business over a period of time

b. THE CORPORATE LEDGER OF ACCOUNTS

1. The relationship of your ledger of accounts to your business plan

Start your financial planning with a serious review of your ledger of accounts and your regular monthly accounting statement presentation. Right now is the best opportunity you will ever have to set a management information standard for your business that allows you to fully monitor business activity.

Many companies fail to grasp the significance of the ledger breakdown in relation to the reporting flexibility it can provide. Think of the actual process of expense allocation. Accounting packages slot information so that output reports can be arranged in virtually any format that individual managers require. Over the years, I have repeatedly seen company executives astounded when an ambitious young accountant offers "new" management reports that give the boss quality information. If the account ledger is properly set up and your accountant is well versed in contemporary programming, you can constantly raise the standard of your financial report breakdowns as your company grows. In most cases, a manager can set out on a blank piece of paper the financial data and the format he or she requires periodically and the accountant can build the report format into his or her system in a matter of hours — but only if the original account ledger breakdown allows for it.

The relevance of your ledger of accounts to the business plan may not be obvious, but they are two ends of the same rainbow. The forecast data of business plans must eventually be linked to detailed operating budgets and management statements, and those are directly affected by the quality of your ledger of accounts. For example, if your administrative expenditures are 20% over budget in the next 6 months and you want to know why, you must review detailed expense breakdowns. Statements that include 20 or 30 different expense accounts and their original anticipated expenditures will help readily identify problem areas much faster than a statement with 6 expenses shown under 6 headings. Detailed examination of these accounts is now a simple thing, too, with computerized programs available to do a lot of the work.

These detailed budgets don't need to be a part of the business plan. However, once you have been taken seriously, based on your business plan, the next level of analysis by financiers will involve a review of your inner workings. The existence of detailed, well-conceived statements could be what helps close the deal. Because analysts work with numbers and statements all the time, they rarely see financial packages that meet their own standards. Surprise them, and at the same time, get your management information system off to a good start.

2. The accounting/non-accounting interface

I have rarely seen a business environment where accountants and their workmates are truly on the same page. I believe that one main reason for this lies in the low priority given to establishing a company's ledger of accounts. Accounting systems tend to gather information over a minimum of two years to develop comparative statements, so once the data collection process is in place, there is a built-in reluctance to change it. After all, if you try to change things next year, it will distort year-to-year comparisons. The terms "accounting" and "distortion" don't go well together.

Accounting packages also allow for the insertion of budget numbers before real world activity and thus become an excellent planning tool. Properly emphasized departments in a company would participate in the creation of the account ledger in areas that might affect them. Take for example the sales manager of a company that both manufactures product and distributes product for other manufacturers. Monitoring sales costs for the two categories would necessitate the ability to distinguish expenses into separate pigeonholes. Before defining a final ledger of accounts, the company accountants had best listen to the sales manager's specific information needs.

The same applies to all situations where an individual manager is responsible for budgetary expenses. Working with such personnel to lay out a report format that is meaningful to them and/or training them to extract information from financial reports will prove invaluable in the long run.

Let's do a reality check. When a new venture is at hand and optimistic entrepreneurs are champing at the bit to enter the fray, who is going to give high priority to accounting ledgers? The business will ultimately be far more manageable if somebody does.

3. Choosing the right accounting package

General accounting software packages that can be used on personal computers are extremely economical for small companies. However, be sure to purchase one that allows you to set up a detailed listing of expense and revenue accounts. Try to anticipate your long-term analytical needs before you decide on a particular package.

This is particularly important if you have departmental statements or well-defined areas in your operation with different managers responsible for performance. Try to envisage your company five years from now and how its operations may be structured. Work with your accountant to draft report formats that give sound information on department performance to the managers. This includes both profit-oriented departments and pure expense departments like product development groups. If you see one or two areas as particularly critical to success, establish enough accounts to support a range of reporting formats.

All accounting packages allow for the comparison of current and prior year results and most include the ability to insert detailed budget data on a monthly basis. If you do not detail things now and try to modify as you grow, you will never be able to generate accurate comparisons to prior years.

A vast array of accounting packages are available, some specialized by industry, others more general in scope. One of the more flexible options comes from two software packages acquired by Computer Associates for full North American distribution. The ACCPAC and Bedford Accounting Systems both originated in Vancouver, Canada, and accommodate both Canadian and U.S. accounting needs. Computer Associates, a large American software house, has now set out to make the systems compatible so that small companies that buy the very economical Bedford system will have the option of easily converting to ACCPAC as the company grows. One-day training sessions will familiarize any bookkeeper with the basics of installing these products.

I have always preferred two sets of four-column reports for management purposes. The first set will compare current month to budget and year-to-date to budget. The second set, where applicable, will compare current to previous year.

4. Setting up your system

As important as having the right program is setting up the procedure by which data is entered into your accounting system. If you set up a ledger of accounts, your administration staff must be trained to allocate accurately so that management reports are not distorted.

To help you review your existing ledger of accounts or build a new one, Worksheet #16 sets some guidelines. However, this is best done in conjunction with an experienced accountant who knows your industry and your company. Ultimately, the best way for you to handle this exercise is to think of it in terms of report needs. Identify the information you need to enhance the running of your business now and as you grow, and charge your accounting staff with the process of ensuring you receive that information on a timely and accurate basis.

I suggest that you provide for report formats that summarize all of your overhead areas (e.g., administrative, marketing, product development), as well as a full breakdown of labor costs by function. Once this is done, you can allocate these expenses against your production and revenue departments proportionately to better understand performance levels.

The first step in financial planning, then, is to work with your accountant to isolate the report information that you will need to manage your business in the future. The package will include detailed reports where necessary as well as summary reports. Some industries, such as the hotel business, adopt a "uniform system of accounts" which is recommended for use by all major properties as it allows for comparative industry or chain data to be consistently developed and measured. For daily management, this may be inadequate unless there are further breakdowns of individual profit centers. If a hotel has five food and beverage facilities and lumps product costs, service and kitchen labor, condiments, entertainment, and promotion into a single statement, it is impossible to measure performance of specific operations. Sub-statements are critical.

While it is by no means a rigid set of accounts, I have listed a full set of department reports for a major hotel operation that I managed in Texas years ago to illustrate a reasonable level of management detail. These appear in Appendix 2 and may be helpful to review before tackling the worksheets in this chapter.

c. DEVELOPMENT COSTS

In an accounting sense, true development costs are like prepaid expenses. As you would with insurance, for example, it is logical that you allocate prepaid expenses over the period of time they cover. This is the same with depreciable assets; the tangible value is expensed over time, usually long after cash payment is complete, as the useful life diminishes.

Since the phrases "development companies" or "technology companies" have emerged, much controversy has centered around the financial treatment of the costs associated with technical and market development. On one hand, these expenses are hardly reflective of the actual operating expenses of traditional profit-motivated departments. Sales groups selling software or engineered products are not responsible for the expenses tied to development of new programs. Likewise, if new products require front-end investment to set up distribution, product literature, market testing, and general market research, these costs have little to do with current sales performance. Logically, in financial reports from departments with specific sales and profit goals, costs of development should be separated.

On the other hand, conservative analysts maintain that showing these development costs as assets on a balance sheet to be amortized over time is not prudent because the expenses have little tangible value and overstate the actual book value of the company. They want such expenses written off as incurred so that development companies show major losses in the early years. This approach gained more popularity after many computer companies succumbed in the early 1970s with rapid technology change and the liquidation value of development assets proved minimal.

Both arguments have merit, and I recommend that two separate department statements, with associated account ledgers, be created for the product and market development expenses associated with business expansion programs. Within this structure, all authorized development projects will have separate ledger accounts for their engineering and marketing expenses up to the point where they are fully integrated into the company product line.

This technique clearly identifies the break between development and regular operations and allows all analysts to treat the expenses according to their own criteria. Also, the method draws attention to the key aspect of your plan. Many investors will be highly influenced by the clarity of your development program presentation. Remember that these people are evaluating your future and by clearly showing the development process you will win bonus points.

Worksheets #16 to #19 are aimed at organizing your financial presentation layout and tying it to your account ledger. Do them now after reading the accompanying comments.

Using Worksheet #16: Summary of Financial Presentation Data

The emphasis in financial forecasting lies with the income and cash flow projections rather than the balance sheet. Ideally, your lead statement, a summary of all operations, will illustrate both profit and cash flow projections for the next five years. There are no hard and fast rules governing presentation, but the idea is to provide the single sheet that will give the busy investor "a quick look at the numbers." These numbers must be detailed enough to impress, but light enough that the reader will want to turn the page.

To accomplish this, I have developed a presentation technique that isolates operating profit details in a secondary role. The financial statements included in the business plan shown in Appendix 1 illustrate this. There, Table 1 is broken into two segments: effect of operations on corporate income and effect of operations on corporate cash flow. This format allows for an attractive profit presentation, a means of recognizing the level to which cash flow will lag behind revenue (i.e., receivables buildup), and an introduction to the expected cash demands of product/market development. Operating forecasts for individual departments show up in Table 2 of the business plan.

To accomplish theses goals, your presentation must—

(a) Summarize the various divisional sources of operating profit and provide a corporate total

(b) Show total corporate overheads (These administrative expenses will be detailed in a separate statement.)

(c) Summarize any non-operating revenues (e.g., interest income) and expenses and calculate projected taxable income

(d) Show the opening cash balance in part 2 of the statement

(e) Formulate a projected cash flow position based on operating profits above

(f) Recognize net non-operating cash flow

(g) Introduce the expected application of funds to develop new products and markets (these development costs will be discussed in detail in the next section)

(h) Include any support footnotes needed to clarify the above

WORKSHEET #16

SUMMARY OF FINANCIAL PRESENTATION DATA

Our company has_______________ profit centers, namely ___________________________________

____

____

____

Our company includes the following overhead departments that do not generate revenue:

____

____

____

Non-operating sources of revenue/cash and demands on cash include:

____

We have/have not tax losses of _______________ to carry forward and apply against operating income and our resulting tax costs next year will be at a rate of _______________%.

Terms of payment by customers in our business affect our cash flow as we expand in the following ways:

____

____

____

Our balance sheet accounts including inventory buildup, purchase of new fixed assets, and liability reductions will demand use of cash in the following areas: ____

____

____

____

____

An increase in supplier credit will reduce the need for cash by ____________________________

____

____

Our development program includes ______________________ product development projects and their associated market development costs. Total planned costs for these areas are __________________and

____

The net effect of the above may result in a format like the following:

Operating profit — Dept. A	xxxxxxx
Operating profit — Dept. B	xxxxxxx
Operating profit — Dept. C	xxxxxxx
Total gross operating profit	xxxxxxx
Corporate administration overheads	xxxxxxx
Marketing overheads	xxxxxxx
Net operating profit	xxxxxxx
Interest income/expense	xxxxxxx
Non-recurring income expense	xxxxxxx
Taxable income	xxxxxxx
Opening cash position	xxxxxxx
Estimated cash flow	
from operations	xxxxxxx
Non-operating cash flow	xxxxxxx
Adjusted asset/liability usage	xxxxxxx
Product development budget	xxxxxxx
Market development budget	xxxxxxx
Closing cash position	xxxxxxx
Planned investor distribution	xxxxxxx

Using Worksheet #17: Operating Department Statement Formats

Financial tables in your business plan will provide support details for each profit center that had an operating result isolated at the beginning of Worksheet #16. The format will vary among businesses, but in all cases it should

WORKSHEET #17
OPERATING DEPARTMENT STATEMENT FORMATS

Department name: ______________________________

The lead source of revenue in this department is ______________________________
____

The relationship between this and other revenues may be described as follows: ______________
____
____

Will these revenue classes grow at the same rate? Why? ______________________________
____
____

Cost of goods sold for each revenue class is ______________________________
____

In comparing our gross profit margin to other industry members we expect to ______________
____

We justify this on the following basis: ______________________________
____
____

In addition to direct labor of ______________ included in cost of goods sold we will have overhead management labor of ______________ in this department. Other major overhead expenses include ______________________________

The expenses most difficult to predict include: ______________________________
____

To improve our forecasts in this department we must ______________________________
____
____
____
before completing this business plan.

isolate the direct labor and materials cost components from other general operating expenses and include divisional overheads. Two examples are included here to show the options. Refer to the Rooms and Food and Beverage departments of Appendix 2 and Table 2, Appendix 1.

Try to break down your revenue sources within each department. Many manufacturers, for example, present an unclear picture if they lump their own product with product supplements they may distribute at lower profit margins. In fact, a good way to present revenue and cost of sales is to group revenue within distinct profit margins and detail related costs of goods sold and their associated gross profit rate.

Distinguish department overhead from corporate overhead. Many statements fail to acknowledge that a portion of overhead is directly attributable to the existence and size of a department. Determine if such a distinction is relevant to your business.

Present your statement in such a way that the bottom line operating profit result exactly equals the amount shown as division or department operating profit in the summary table.

Keep in mind that you are attempting to develop formula relationships between expenses and revenue and establish a means for the "economies of scale" to gradually lead to higher profit margins. This is one argument that is always easy to make and it greatly reduces the input time in your spreadsheet development if many of the expense budgets are directly related to revenue targets. For example, you may determine that your expected material costs in production will equal 32% of sales in the first year and decline 1% per year as volume grows. Labor costs, shipping, advertising budgets, and installation costs may bear similar relationships. Other fixed costs like rent, auto leases, or contract janitorial services may not be affected by revenue. Where possible, develop defendable formulas and keep them close at hand if you are required to verbally verify financial data in the plan.

Using Worksheet #18: Corporate Overhead Statements

Corporate overhead represents the expenses that you cannot normally tie to a single department. It tends to cover all general administrative, legal, and other expenses and costs incurred by senior management to advance the long-term goals of the company and maintain a satisfactory business environment for corporate growth.

Business analysts are keenly interested in how you conduct your executive affairs. This is where they determine if you are running "lean and mean"

WORKSHEET #18

CORPORATE OVERHEAD STATEMENTS

Executive salaries for the first year of business total ______________________________.
Of this approximately______________ % can be applied directly to production costs, ___________% can be applied directly to sales expenses, and ______________% to development costs.

Summarize a justification for all major expenditures and their relevance.

Summarize contractual commitments such as lease terms, equipment obligations, and professional retainers.

Estimate the volume of business this overhead level can handle before any major increase in space is required.

or "fat and comfortable." Try to be miserly in this area. Any expenses associated with development should not be shown here. If you or a senior person is also very involved in development projects, allocate that time to the development cost budget. Do the same for related travel costs. Any expenses incurred by a corporate group on behalf of specific departments should be allocated and appear in department listings rather than being lumped with general overhead. Try to avoid use of miscellaneous accounts where possible as they are frowned upon.

The same rules apply to corporate marketing and market development. Direct selling costs are not a part of marketing overhead and all costs directly attributable to a specific selling process belong under cost of goods sold. Project costs related to developing a new market as an authorized corporate investment also deserve to be isolated from any general overhead accounts.

Note: In small companies, it is a mistake to present a grand management team of well-paid support strategists who make no direct contribution to profitability. You must walk a fine line. You need names and reputations that show the ability to handle growth, but you don't need the cost of excess MBA brain power.

Using Worksheet #19: Development Department Statements

There are four basic categories of development functions that most corporate activity will fall into:

(a) *Pure research and development:* This is normally reserved for large companies like DuPont or 3M who let researchers freewheel within their realm of expertise.

(b) *Product development:* This is more common in smaller companies where a specific market niche is targeted and the development group aims to refine a design or apply proven technology to fill the market void.

All expenses related to prototype fall into this category. While marketing personnel may provide a service to the product development group by identifying sites to place prototypes, these are actually product development costs. This distinction is particularly important in jurisdictions where research and development costs are eligible for tax credits. It can save you money. Often, product development can be funded but there is no support for market development.

WORKSHEET #19

DEVELOPMENT DEPARTMENT STATEMENTS

List all authorized development projects, the projected date of completion, estimated product development costs, associated market development budget, estimated sales needed to recover project investment, and expected date this will be achieved. For each project, attach a one-page description showing the relevance to the corporate plans.

Project #/ Description	Completion date	Product development budget	Market development budget	$ sales to break even	Break-even date

Describe the relationship of all projects and any interdependence. Is there a critical path of completion dates necessary to achieve goals and meet budgets?

____

____

____

____

____

____

____

____

____

____

(c) *Market development:* This relates to a specific start-up strategy to research and test markets.

(d) *Corporate development:* If a company has a specific corporate expansion team dedicated to mergers, acquisitions, acquisition of licensing or distribution rights, or real estate investment, it may function within a separate development department and budget. This is not common in most small companies.

Worksheet #19 addresses issues related to product and market development. As previously mentioned, a good way to present a summary of expenses is by project. In your ledger of accounts you can incorporate standard project accounts and allot account number space for a group of projects. In other words, each project may have ten sub-accounts to provide a total project cost to date. While project managers may get detailed lists of expenses to monitor, the summary report for development would only show one total per project.

d. FUNDING STRUCTURES AND THEIR APPLICATION

In the Executive Summary, the readers of your business plan are normally introduced to your funding needs and are given an overview of your proposed investment structure. By the time they reach the financial plan segment of the presentation, those readers are much more familiar with details of your business operation, your marketing and sales plan, and your financial forecasts and budgets. It is time for a concise presentation of the investment proposal.

There are three critical considerations when you develop a specific financial structure for a business funding program:

(a) the jurisdictional requirements of relevant government regulatory bodies;

(b) the dilution effect and costs attached to the debt/equity nature of the financing instruments; and

(c) how expansion financing will influence your managerial control of the company.

In each of these areas, there are some straightforward ways to reduce the demands of the two things you never have enough of: time and money.

1. Minimize the cost of meeting regulatory criteria: Remain a private company

Being a private company is much less demanding than being a public company. Many business managers associate going public with success and image. In truth, it is an expensive, time-consuming process that makes you accountable to a wide range of people. Public trading of shares offers only one constant, direct advantage: liquidity. Many times a second advantage occurs when the market value of shares creates a defined measure of goodwill value for the company. Naturally, this can help set pricing for new issues or collateral value for additional borrowing of funds. However, the opposite effect can occur when bear market conditions drop the market value below book value for many shares, thus reducing the ability to find new financing. Most small companies, intent on uninterrupted management of a growth business, should exhaust all private financing avenues first and go public on one of the junior exchanges only as a last resort.

In many jurisdictions, any broad solicitation for corporate funding demands the filing of an Offering Memorandum or Financial Prospectus. However, if you are seeking a small group of investors for your enterprise, many states and provinces allow for the unregistered solicitation of sophisticated investors. Normally you are restricted to 25 to 100 investors and each must have a minimum buying power of $25,000 or more depending on the prevailing laws. Check with the governing body in your area.

If you are planning to recruit investors and are uncertain about the solicitation restrictions you face, there are two phrases that will come in handy. Once the business plan is packaged and ready for release, stamp "Confidential — For Internal Use Only" and/or "Draft — For Discussion Purposes Only" on the front cover and title page. Such unofficial documents can pique the curiosity of potential investors far more easily than official memorandums and provide a more intimate pursuit of funding support. In addition, they allow you the flexibility to approach potential investors within the bounds of the law.

Always include some basic disclaimer with your financial presentation: THERE IS NO REPRESENTATION MADE IN CONNECTION WITH THIS PLAN THAT FINANCIAL PROJECTIONS WILL BE ACHIEVED OR THAT ASSUMPTIONS WILL REMAIN CONSTANT.

The tone in which the financial plan is presented is also important. If you are seeking a single major investor, it is best to present your tentative financial structure as a basis for discussion. Demonstrate that you can be sensitive to structural requirements of a lead investor and are willing to consider alternative proposals if the dollar investment is significant.

2. Equity dilution versus the cost of debt

The simplest investment proposal offers the funding source the opportunity to buy shares at a fixed price and assume all the rewards, rights, and risks of existing shareholders. This avenue is not taken as often as you may think unless a public offering is pending in the near future.

One common alternative is an offer of common stock without voting rights. The rationale here is that investors achieve the same return on investment as regular shareholders but have less power to affect corporate policy at annual general meetings. Management likes non-voting shares, and many private, passive investors are attracted to receiving shares at a slight discount (often around 6% to 10%) to surrender a power they will likely never use.

For the company, the main attraction of common shares is that there is no obligation to pay dividends or guarantee cash flow to the investor in the short term. Growth-oriented small companies must provide some general scenario (usually verbally rather than in writing) that shows investors when they will be able to liquidate their investment and how. This could be through a public offering, sale to a larger company, or share buy-back plan by the company.

Preferred shares, with a guaranteed preferred rate of dividend payment ranking ahead of common shares, are also used as an investment vehicle. This halfway approach to debt financing is not without merit in some circumstances. However, many growth companies are reluctant to take on fixed cash payments while internal needs are high.

Outright debt is rarely used to finance high-risk companies because the limited return holds little appeal to investors. The popular compromise for both company and investor is often convertible debt (i.e., a loan that can be converted to straight equity over a certain period of time). The attraction to investors is that their money is more secure than that of the common shareholders, but they can convert at a mutually recognized premium at some point in the future.

For example, say that a company's common shares have a current value estimated at $2.20 per share. If they are raising $250,000.00, they may agree to a 10% convertible debenture. If exercised within a year, the holder would receive 100,000 shares (based on conversion share price of $2.50 per share), and if exercised in the second year, they may receive 85,000 shares (based on a conversion price of $2.85 per share). The longer the debenture holder delays the commitment to equity participation, the higher the price that is paid. After a certain term, the conversion option may lapse and the payment of the debt would begin based on pre-arranged terms.

Other popular investment plans include options and warrants. These instruments provide the incentive for today's investors to increase their position under favorable terms in the future. With no commitment to provide additional investment down the road, the investor gains the right to buy more shares at his or her option. This is particularly useful to a company that wants to raise money in two or more stages.

If an investor buys 10,000 shares at $2.20 each now, the attached warrant or option may allow him or her to buy another 10,000 at $2.50 within a year or $2.85 within two years.

Creative financial structuring can benefit all parties. Historically, I have found that good tax lawyers have to be on top of the best options available to a greater extent than accountants, but this varies in different cities. Structuring your deal, once you know exactly how much money you need, is a critical step. The one thing you do not want to surrender is managerial control.

3. Maintaining managerial control

Most investors want you to want control. Their judgment of you, the business champion, will be as important as their assessment of the business plan. They will expect a proposal that gives you effective, if not outright, control of the company. This is not to say that major investors will not insist on terms that protect their investment. If you get in trouble, they will expect the right to step in. In other words, large investments are often tied to performance clauses.

Many company owners bent on expansion fail to understand effective control as the critical issue. They are blind to any agreement where they relinquish more than 49% of outstanding common shares. In technical companies in particular, this is often a red herring. Controlling the majority of the board of directors, management contracts, self-designated share options, control of group voting rights, administration of employee stock plans, or fragmented shareholder groups all offer a means to maintaining effective control. Many companies' destinies remain in the hands of one leader who actually owns as little as 10% of the company.

Still, in the age of hostile takeovers and corporate raiders, a little prudence is wise. This is why structures that stagger dilution (i.e., convertible debt) are appealing. In my mind, the best single vehicle for a company confident in its future adds one additional wrinkle to a convertible offer: a redemption feature.

A convertible, redeemable debenture limits the potential upside of the investor at the option of the company. In your initial proposal, consider including the following term: "At any time the company reserves the right to redeem all outstanding debentures by a buy-out payment that gives the debenture holder an annualized return of 25% on all outstanding principal."

In other words, once you have earned your investors that kind of return, you are free to refinance and short circuit their conversion option, which eliminates pending equity dilution.

Worksheet #20 will help set your investment structure.

e. SHARE VALUATION

A logical part of any investment discussion is a brief discourse on how you arrived at your share valuation. The price that you will ask for your shares should recognize that risk takers want their 35% to 65% annualized return when the chance to liquidate arises. The business plan shown in Appendix 1 goes to great length to describe its pricing rationale simply as a matter for discussion. No promises are made and acceptable price/earnings ratios help illustrate the attractiveness of the share offer.

If this segment of your plan is produced with professionalism and controlled optimism, it can serve as an excellent selling influence. Always include appropriate disclaimers.

Using Worksheet #20: Drafting an Investment Structure

All of the implications of risk and reward now come into play for both you and the investor. It is standard practice in new share offerings to allow all current shareholders the right to maintain their pro rata undiluted equity position if they wish to respond to a new offering.

Setting share price or interest terms on convertible debt is a complicated issue. In public offerings where a brokerage firm distributes the issue (either with guaranteed or nonguaranteed results), the selling price is a point of negotiation between the stockbroker and the company. In private issues, it is left more to the discretion of the company to establish worth and define the terms under which it will sell shares.

WORKSHEET #20

DRAFTING AN INVESTMENT STRUCTURE

Our current outstanding common shares number______________________________
and major shareholdings include: ____

Previous shares have been allocated at the following price on the described dates _______________

The net book value per share, based on our latest balance sheet equals _______________/share.
We feel that we can justify a goodwill factor of ____________/share based on _______________

We propose to issue equity/debt financing instruments on the following terms: _______________

Assuming full equity dilution, we expect our earnings per share in each of the next five years to equal ___

On the basis of this offering we are expecting to seek total net funding of __________________
while diluting current shareholder equity by __________________%.

Aside from price, the other main consideration in the terms of the share/debt offer is the implication of partial completion. Your business plan is based on raising a specified amount of money, and if you are only half successful, this may affect the attractiveness of the investment. You have to decide the terms of purchase. Can the buyer of shares withdraw if the total offering is not completed? The added risk of partial completion will vary with your planned use of funds. If priorities are set for fund uses and a quarter of funding is less critical than the first 75%, you may stipulate in your proposal that all funds will be held in trust until 75% of the issue is committed.

It is up to you to set the tentative terms of investment and cover any potentially contentious points. Make sure that earnings per share estimates are based on the expected number of shares outstanding during that year.

6
THE TEAM PROFILE

a. DEFINING YOUR TEAM

If your business is of a size where you *are* the team, this section has little application other than the need for you to document your talents to cover all elements of the business. An in-depth personal resume and references will have to suffice. Do recognize, however, that the dependence of the business on you alone may concern any major investor, supplier, or customer. In this case, your entire business is built on your character. Unless you have personal collateral to support financing, it is unlikely that you will receive professional financing. Private individual financing will depend heavily on your ability to sell yourself and your durability. This section assumes businesses will have not only a leader, but a team.

Do not center your business plan around the fact that you are a critical element to success. Let readers deduce that for themselves — if it is true. The ideal business entity, from the investor viewpoint at least, can survive the departure of anyone.

It takes a mature, confident individual (the kind most investors would like to back) to develop a business strategy that precludes an eternal need for his or her services. Ego is a common denominator among successful entrepreneurs. Keep yours under control. Remember that the objective at hand is to illustrate the appeal and potential of a business, not one or two human beings. Even if you are a superstar, the investment assessment will evaluate you largely in terms of the team you play for. Is it capable of a championship year?

Good teams are balanced: they have specialists and utility players, they have seasoned veterans and agile rookies, they have offensive threats and a stable defense. Occasionally they bench a starter and bring in a rising star or make a trade. As important as the merits of individual team members is the chemistry of the group.

In a brief written summary, you can only hope to extol the more tangible attributes of key people. Efforts to describe positive group chemistry are usually fruitless unless you are willing to stand out from the crowd. We all know that there is risk attached to being the exception, but I think that you have to do something unique to help highlight your personnel. I will loudly applaud the first business plan I see where the team captain and fellow managers dress in basketball or baseball uniforms and pose around a trophy in the format normally reserved for champions.

For a moment, place yourself in the role of the professional investors who will read your business plan, maybe their fortieth this month. If they have little or no direct contact with the business, evaluating the people based purely on written description is very difficult. A half-page précis of degrees and experience tells such a small part of the story. If your key people are a reasonably healthy, energetic, bright-looking group, hire a professional photographer and get a top quality shot — and I stress quality. Either use the sports angle mentioned above or show individuals in their work environment, not sitting around a boardroom.

The three key aspects of your description of corporate management are organizational structure, operating management personnel, and, in many cases, the board of directors.

b. TEAM MEMBERS AND THEIR RELATIONSHIP

1. Organization

A simple organization chart for a small business must identify all of the key management functions and how they interrelate. Normally, the chief executive officer (CEO) has three to five key people reporting directly to him or her. These people cover the roles of marketing, sales, product engineering, manufacturing or operations management, and finance and administration. In spite of some of the idealistic theories that have evolved on team decision-making in recent years, guard carefully against too much management by committee. Companies are, at best, benevolent dictatorships, not democracies.

A simple organizational structure suitable to most smaller entities might be as shown in the diagram below.

The exact nature of your business will dictate the ideal blend of in-house full-time expertise versus specialized external support. In my opinion, the common bias toward recruiting full-time senior management for some critical business functions is ill-founded. The associated overhead can drain limited finances and lead to make-work projects if the need for the expertise is cyclical.

An example of this is the dilemma that can face any company that sets out to apply a technology and take the prototype into production. The expertise attached to developing a technical product specification is distinct from talent required to package that product for mass distribution. Rarely are the two abilities found in one individual. Do you require two key people within the company? Likely not.

Consider recruiting an external production and product design specialist as a key project participant. Agree to retain this person or group under contractual terms that clearly commit him or her to your program.

Separate all the elements of your business operation that are project oriented from those that are continuous. Certainly, sales management, for instance, is ongoing and requires a dedicated in-house person. Market analysis, however, might be a periodic task best allocated to an outside specialist. Extra effort to interview and recruit stable, highly regarded expert associates can help fill in a shallow management team.

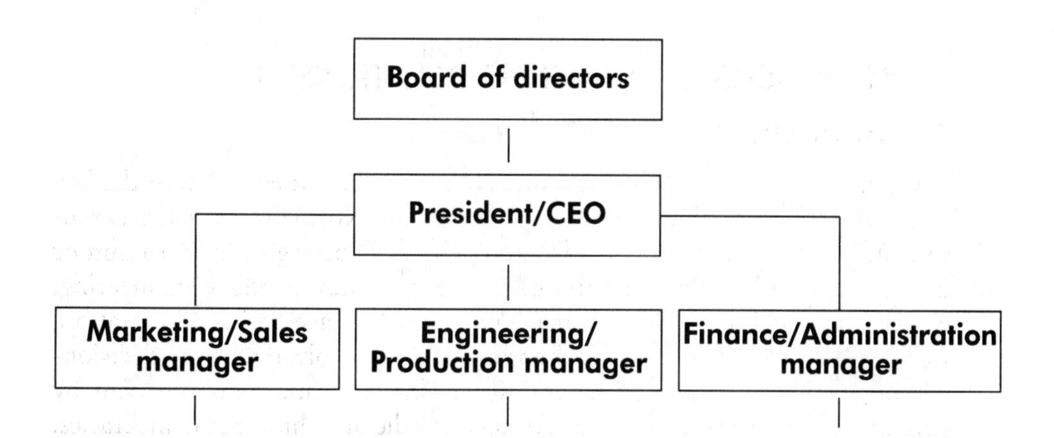

Where these functions are vital to success, build them into the third level of your organizational structure and present the experts as a part of your team.

2. Operating management

Start-up businesses often face one major people problem: commonality. The principals look the same, think the same, and have the same experience base. What starts as compatibility can soon turn to conflict when gaps in overall expertise harm the business. While a common thread of business philosophy, morality, and purpose are appealing in a management team, too much common experience is a drawback.

Review the resumes of key people and assess the overall scope of your team. Each key manager must have proven success and experience in his or her field of responsibility. Try to be consistent in the level of detail presented on all personnel, but don't bulk up the summary to compensate for a lack of degrees or experience if one or two team members are short of formal training. Some of the best sales people and most pragmatic technicians have never been inside a university and you have nothing to apologize for if they are right for your team.

3. Board of directors and/or advisory boards

The idea of soliciting outside directors to round out a full business strategy team has gained wide popularity in recent years. Adding a few high-profile names to your roster certainly helps attract attention, but you should offer such positions selectively. Professional directors are not that hard to find and many mean well if they participate in an active board bent on steering the corporate ship.

I have seen this concept work and I have seen it fail miserably. Boards of small companies normally have three, five, or seven directors with the founding management well represented. Start up financiers also expect representation. Because it is the mandate of the board to represent all shareholders and monitor the progress of management, anybody who takes on this position inherits a major responsibility. In many jurisdictions, that responsibility is becoming more onerous as directors are held more accountable by the courts and media for the actions of their companies. For this reason, I have concluded that the day of name directors is disappearing. All directors should have a vested financial interest in the company and share the commitment of the shareholders they represent.

You can expect to see more companies with advisory boards to supplant the void of big-name directors. Advisory boards consist of paid professionals who do not want the risk of being a director but are attracted by the growth potential of a company. Retired industry leaders and active experts from the periphery of your business can lend name, support, and expertise to you under a clear advisory board mandate not distorted by the legal priorities of the board of directors.

The one common denominator of these two boards is that they link with the internal management team through the CEO and that they are primarily support groups to help reach management objectives. They are less informed on the intricacies of daily company life than is management, but they are often more capable of standing back and viewing the big picture.

Worksheet #21 provides a means of setting the status of your team. This includes recognition of all operational and advisory roles and their current status.

Using Worksheet #21: Describing the Team

The layout of this worksheet is set to determine both what you have and what you need. If you do not have people officially on staff, but they have made tentative commitments to join when you secure suitable financing, this should be stated. Minimize the uncertainties of recruitment by taking as many steps as possible to nail down the team.

Throughout the development of your business plan, do everything possible to reduce uncertainties and attach names and faces to key positions. Good people are not easy to find for most businesses, and if your plan relies on your ability to go out and find a brilliant electronics engineer and an international sales manager who knows the European and Asian marketplace, then you had better have some specific people tentatively committed.

Do not compromise on qualifications of specialists or advisers based on local availability. Remember that on paper it is the impressiveness of the individual's background that is the issue, not his or her residence.

Strive for a sense of variety and worldliness in the group. Make sure your advisers cover all the key disciplines of finance, production, marketing, and administration and have an experience base in your marketplace. Can they help chart the financial destiny of the company and open doors to future economic, social, and political needs of the company?

WORKSHEET #21

DESCRIBING THE TEAM

List the names, positions, and major attributes of key operations people fully committed to the project:

List names, positions, attributes, and outstanding issues of key operating people *conditionally committed* to the project:

Identify key positions as yet unfilled:

Describe the board of directors and/or advisory board and what they bring to the company:

Do you have well-documented resumes for all key personnel?

What voids exist in your group experience base relative to the task ahead? Can they be filled by external specialists?

Strive to have your position described as follows: "The CEO has a strong board to work with, solid senior management personnel in place, and a couple of real up-and-comers waiting in the wings."

c. ATTRACTING AND KEEPING THE RIGHT PEOPLE

The brief profiles of key personnel that you include in the team segment of your business plan are comparable to a financial balance sheet in that they freeze the makeup of your organization at a point in time. For analysts of the plan, they must project what will happen to the people dynamics of your company through the next five years. In other words, in the same manner that they review the practicality of your revenue and expense projections, they will assess your strategy and incentives to keep your team happy, motivated, and productive.

If your business base is technological, they will rate your internal vulnerability to confidentiality problems and security leaks. They will rate the depth of your group and your ability to withstand the sudden departure of a senior staff member. They will try to determine whether you understand that everybody involved must profit from the success of your operation.

While there is no room to go into great detail in your plan, the main issue is to acknowledge and describe how you have dealt with the need to both motivate and stabilize your team. Profit sharing and/or stock option incentives for key people are the most common economic motivators and well-conceived employment contracts are sound stabilizers. The challenge of both is to structure arrangements to perpetuate a healthy attitude.

1. Equity incentives

In young businesses, I have seen ill-conceived front-end incentives dangled before managers who proved disastrous within six months. In one case, the entire equity incentive equalling 12% of the company was loaded on the front end and the buy back to eliminate the problem executive proved very expensive. Terms related to such earned equity arrangements should always be spread over a minimum of two years.

Stock options are most popular in companies that are planning to go public in the future and in situations where there are attractive personal tax advantages to the option holder who stands to make capital gains or build a tangible asset over time. There are numerous formulas that make sense, but in small companies, I think equity participation should be reserved for key management and technicians.

The other aspect to deal with is who has the option: the company or the employee. The preferable corporate stance is a basic "sweat equity" package where a percentage of remuneration is made in the form of equity. In other words, the company can function with less cash because it pays only a portion of salary to senior managers in the form of cash. In addition, if the employee leaves or is terminated, the sweat equity agreement provides the company with a means of buying out the ex-employee under viable terms and conditions.

2. Profit sharing

The only problem with profit sharing in small companies is that it holds management accountable to all profit sharers to reveal profit calculations. Many entrepreneurs do not like that.

A profit pool equal to 10% of net income before tax can only be illustrated through a full review of the income statement. For this reason, some incentive programs are tied more directly to sales or gross profit margins.

Sales management, for example, may have incentives tied to a bonus based on exceeding target sales where the target should generate a base level of profit. Production management, on the other hand, may earn incentives attached to their responsibility for achieving a target direct cost per unit manufactured. This more complex method of motivating specific managers isolates their performance goals in accordance with their areas of responsibility. The onus falls on the general manager to control overheads to achieve overall profit.

In the business plan, you will simply summarize the basics of your stock option or profit-sharing plans, but in most cases their existence will be viewed as a plus for your business program. The only concern will be if the package is seen as too generous or inconsistent in application to the point of creating resentment.

3. Employment contracts

A stable management, sales, and production group can save a company a lot of money. Within reason, it is a large part of the ownership challenge to provide positive conditions for all employees. Most senior managers view the existence of an employment contract, formal or informal, as an attractive thing.

All good contracts are two-way streets. For the company, a formal agreement can clearly outline all restrictions against disclosure of proprietary company information. Although it is often impossible to fully restrict an employee from leaving and using your customer lists and production data to become a competitor, a good employment contract can provide a stiff deterrent. Such contracts do not stop you from terminating an executive for cause but do establish a pay out method. They also detail terms of equity buy back for stockholders.

All major stockholders who are active in the company should also have employment contracts that distinguish their operating roles from their equity positions. Very often companies outgrow the expertise of founding members and the result is an awkward confrontation when partners stand in conflict. Either by separate agreement or as part of their employment contracts, founding partners should have a means of dealing with a potential schism.

The best method is some form of "shotgun clause," so called because any senior partner can pull the trigger. The simplest form occurs when one partner notifies the others of a desire to end the relationship. By so doing, this person is offering to either buy out the business or sell his or her share. Once the other partners are notified of this wish, they set the value and the first partner can either buy or sell based on this price and a set buy-out period.

A simple twist in this arrangement is where one partner issues the escape notice and also names the price. Then the other partners have the option of buying or selling. It is the cleanest way there is to avoid long legal hassles between diverging forces.

The existence of preconceived arrangements to deal with people issues is often underestimated by first-time entrepreneurs who only see good times ahead for themselves and their associates. Don't kid yourself. Your sensitivities toward people needs and the volatility of human relationships in business can make or break your company.

This module is not suitable for the broad use of worksheets to formulate your position, but Worksheet #22 may help you summarize a brief commentary, even if it is something to be addressed with employees in the future.

4. Employee manuals

All employees should have a clear understanding of company policies and there is no better format than a concise introductory manual that spells out the general terms of employment for everybody in your company. This document should detail everything from holiday policy to grounds for dismissal, employment benefits to dress code.

I suggest that new employees provide a signed copy for corporate personnel records to confirm that they have read and are aware of the content of the company policy manual. Include a brief confidentiality agreement covering all company business.

While such a manual does not appear directly in your business plan, its existence can have an influence on the overall valuation of your business. Good business analysts will explore beyond your business plan before they endorse funding of your program, and you will earn points for showing good communication with employees.

Using Worksheet #22: Team Incentives

There is no need, in the written document, to go into the specific incentives of key people. All that is required is the general criteria on which profit sharing or share option deals are based and the total effect of such plans on profits and equity dilution.

No single employee's incentives should be too far from the norm. Confidential personal incentives have a way of leaking out of personnel files and too much discrepancy can cause animosity. Sales groups are notorious for being disliked by technicians and accountants when they reap large sales incentives. This is an even more serious problem if cost constraints exist in production and administration while the sales force basks in glory.

WORKSHEET #22
TEAM INCENTIVES

Our philosophy of profit sharing and equity options can be described as follows:

The following key people do/will participate in this program:

Currently, the company has employment contracts with

All employees who join our company receive an introductory package which includes:

Our main priority at this time to develop our employee incentives is

7
CONCLUDING REMARKS AND APPENDIXES

a. THE SUMMATION

It is important to end your business plan on a positive note. While the entire thrust of the written report emphasizes a program aimed at success, this brief section offers a final chance to appeal to your investment jury. Like the summation in a courtroom, you consolidate the facts that make your case and conclude with an appeal for the jurors to endorse your logic.

The conclusion should draw directly from information already provided. It is not the time or place to introduce new facts. A direct reiteration of two or three key points from each of the four foundation sections must gel into a cohesive summary of your plan.

A brief expression of appreciation to the reader for taking the time to read your report is a worthwhile gesture. An offer to provide additional information as required also shows a willingness to cooperate.

If you have included appendixes, briefly outline their content and relevance to your conclusions. It is assumed that both your concluding remarks and the appendixes deal with common important issues.

While you should not rely too heavily on enthusiasm, it doesn't hurt to convey a sense of corporate spirit. Leave your reader with the impression that the company is currently building momentum and that the entire management team is solidly behind the business plan.

b. IMPORTANT SUPPLEMENTARY DATA

Every business plan will rely on certain assumptions or special information that is critical to its success. Be it patents, tax opinions, management superstars, or major contracts, the information is vital to the business plan.

In these cases, it is appropriate to add an appendix that supports your position. Consider the following possibilities:

(a) *Audited statements:* Your business plan is based on pro forma information that shows the potential of the business. This must have substance based on current affairs, so a copy of the latest independently prepared financial statement is a common appendix to business plans.

(b) *Management biographies:* Detailed executive resumes are also commonly included at the end of plans. However, rather than pulling old data from personnel files and making copies, an effort should be made to offer a basic package with the resumes in similar formats and with a maximum of two pages per individual.

(c) *Consultant and adviser biographies:* The same rules apply as in the preceding point.

(d) *Key patent and copyright data:* The cover page of a patent or the latest status letter from your patent lawyer on your applications is valuable.

(e) *Timely magazine articles:* Whether they include direct references to your company, technology, competition, or marketplace, publications psychologically legitimize your endeavor. There will always be the "it must be true, I read it in the newspaper" mentality, and this is one place it can work to your advantage.

(f) *Engineering, consultant, or architectural reports:* A professional evaluation of your product design, a marketing report on consumer reaction to your prototype, and renderings or a photo of the scale model of your new hotel all qualify as potential key support data for your plan.

(g) *Major contracts:* If you have a repetitive order on hand to supply AT&T with anything from paint to semiconductors or McDonald's with anything from potatoes to golden arches, a copy of the purchase order might do more than your entire plan to win approval.

(h) *Product literature:* Sometimes included behind your report, literature is more often submitted independently or as a forerunner to the actual presentation of a business plan.

(i) *Internal policy documents:* Under-utilized as an insight into your corporate life, a document that indicates action rather than words can be most effective to stimulate serious interest in the company. Readers may know far less about day-to-day operations of a manufacturing or service business than you think, and such a document can open a door for a more intimate discussion of your business.

(j) *Tax opinion letters:* Tax shelters have become a large part of small-business financing and the fund-raising process is often based on tax treatment options as they apply to the company or the investor. This might deal with capital gains treatment, depreciation rates, transfer of tax credits, or partnership terms.

(k) *List of current shareholders:* This is not too common as many shareholders feel such data is private and often restrict it to major shareholders (more than 10%).

8

THE EXECUTIVE SUMMARY

Although the Executive Summary serves as the introduction to your business plan, and although you will be thinking about its content throughout the process of developing your foundation modules (remember to refer to the information you gathered in chapter 2 in Worksheets #3 and #4), it will probably be the last part of the plan you write because it summarizes the entire plan. The challenge of the Executive Summary is to be concise and precise and to capture the essence of the deal. Your main enemy will be the common tendency to be verbose and general.

The Executive Summary must be tied directly to the business facts that are in the body of the document. While the emphasis, style, and personalized aspects can easily be adapted to a specific audience, all good summaries cover some key points. In making your summary, you should clearly state the following:

(a) Your current status including description of the product and market
(b) Your immediate goals as they relate to current products and markets
(c) Your immediate financial needs
(d) Your five-year goals for product and market development
(e) Your five-year needs to finance the growth of your entire business
(f) The essence of what makes your opportunity unique

Focus attention strictly on the product, marketing plan, personnel, and financial logistics that will make your program work and forget the pet projects, new product ideas, corporate spinoffs, franchise possibilities and the offer from a realtor to sell your company. Don't cloud the issue for the potential investor.

If you establish a firm investment proposal at this stage, I suggest a separate, one-page proposal that clearly outlines the risk and reward structure. Often investors are offered a unit with a fixed price ranging from $5,000 to $100,000 depending on the deal. A unit can consist of one or two classes of common shares (voting and non-voting), preferred stock or convertible debt, and occasionally warrants or options.

There is normally no effort at this stage to justify the asking price for a sale of a small part of the company. The reader must assess the data in the body of your report to make that evaluation. Unit price simply sets the minimum buy-in to participate in the investment and is often established by government securities rules.

Conclude your Executive Summary with a brief introduction to the foundation modules of your report, and invite further enquiries by the reader.

Worksheet #23 is provided as a simple review tool to make sure you cover the necessary topics in your summary.

WORKSHEET #23
THE EXECUTIVE SUMMARY

Have we clearly introduced our company and its business? ______________________

Have we stated both short- and long-term objectives? ______________________

Do we have a mission statement? ______________________

Who is this summary aimed at? ______________________

To which of the major concerns of investors are we vulnerable? ______________________

____

____

Have we anticipated these and addressed these concerns? ______________________

How have we established that our company is unique? ______________________

Can we clearly identify all regulatory procedures undertaken and anticipated to fill our business development needs? ______________________

What are our major product/service strengths? ______________________

____

____

____

What are the main marketplace attractions of this business and how are we responding?

____

____

____

What are our financial strengths and how will new capital help? ______________________

____

____

What is the long-term attraction of this company? ______________________

____

9
PRESENTING AN IMPRESSIVE DOCUMENT

Now that you have gathered all your data and completed all the modules, you are ready to put your business plan together into a package.

a. THE COVERING LETTER

The covering letter plays an important role in your business plan package. It is normally the only part of your presentation that is personalized and, as such, provides a means of tailoring your package to a specific investor or highlighting information of particular interest to your contact. The plan should always be introduced with a personal letter addressed to the person for whom it is intended, even if you hand it to him or her personally.

Follow these four simple rules when preparing your covering letter:

(a) The first paragraph should clearly indicate the reason or terms under which the recipient has been sent this package. If you are delivering it at the request of an intermediary, state so and clarify the relationship as you understand it.

(b) Never include any deeply personal remarks that might preclude a copy of the letter being made for the recipient's colleagues. If you have cause to add a personal remark, put it on a separate piece of paper.

(c) Clarify or summarize your expectations based on any previous discussion in one paragraph, and outline your availability for further discussion.

(d) The final paragraph should suggest the next step and indicate that you will call personally on a specific date to discuss this suggestion. This allows you to control the next move rather than waiting patiently for a response.

Try to confine the letter to a single page; it should never exceed two pages. Consider the examples shown in Samples #1 and #2.

Keep an organized file of all covering letters that have been sent. Recover all copies of the business plan from circulation where possible, and monitor the whereabouts of any floating copies.

If you place copies in the hands of agents who are recruiting financial support, make sure that they abide by your program of documenting distribution. Your plans could find their way into competitors' hands. If you number your distribution copies, you can occasionally trace the source of leaked information if a "rogue copy" of your plan is making the rounds.

b. WRITING STYLE

Coherence and readability are critical in your business plan. For this reason, many business managers recruit professional writers to put the finishing touches on their plans. This can range from a pure editing job of a draft of the plan to the actual complete consolidation of your worksheets into the written plan. Whether you choose to write the document yourself or assign this task to an individual, always review the writing for accuracy and clarity. Also have an outsider, unfamiliar with the details of your business, read and critique, as he or she will find it much easier to identify unclear areas.

If you have little writing experience but intend to take on this challenge yourself, you might wish to refer to the numerous books available in bookstores and libraries on the subject of writing style. Following are some basic points to consider if you do write the plan and other points to consider if you hire a ghostwriter.

1. Writing your own plan

When you write, first make sure you include all key components of your plan and place them in a realistic context.

Next, address the issue of change. While a description of the product and business helps place things in perspective, it does not normally exemplify the real dynamics of the business. You must acknowledge that you are dealing with a living entity that will continue to grow in positive ways. The

SAMPLE #1

COVERING LETTER — EXAMPLE #1

March 1, 200-

J. Smith
123 Any Street
Anytown, Anywhere 78910

Dear Sir or Madam:

Based on a request from our mutual business acquaintance, Ms. Joanna Smith, Manager at the Bank of America, I enclose a copy of our corporate business plan and support material.

Ms. Smith has been a valued supporter of our efforts over the past three years while we have banked at her branch and has agreed to act as a reference to our corporate character.

We are currently seeking a lead investor who can consolidate the required funding for our planned plant expansion and new market development program.

Based on our preliminary research, we feel that this proposal meets the general investment criteria of your company and falls within your preferred initial investment range of $1,000,000 to $5,000,000. We would like to explore a fiscal relationship at your earliest convenience.

The enclosed product video and promotional literature illustrate our current product line and the business plan introduces our full corporate strategy for the next two years and includes five year pro forma financial statements. We have established a proposed investment structure but are open to your suggestions.

I will be flying east next week and hope to meet with you and your associates for preliminary discussions during my visit. If I can provide any further information before Monday please call me or Mr. James Morgan at this office. Otherwise I will contact you prior to my departure to firm up an appointment.

Yours truly,

Joe Smith

Joe Smith

SAMPLE #2

COVERING LETTER — EXAMPLE #2

March 1, 200-

J. Smith
123 Any Street
Anytown, Anywhere 78910

Dear Dr. Jones:

As I mentioned after the golf tournament last month, our company will be entering a fund-raising phase in the near future to support our exciting growth program. This is expected to be our last private placement for some time, and we plan to recruit investors known to principals of the company by offering investment units valued at $30,000.

Details are included in the full business plan document which I have enclosed. Circulation is being restricted to a very small group at this stage on a confidential basis, and I would appreciate it if you would check with me before revealing it to parties other than your accountant as some of the information could assist our competitors if it fell into the wrong hands.

I am planning to host a small gathering of our corporate friends next Thursday evening in our board room to answer questions on the business plan and to demonstrate our next generation of product. We have one prototype model that is going to revolutionize this industry.

After that meeting I am hoping to quickly get a clear picture of the level of investment interest in the immediate community. As we grow our long-term fiscal strategy is to retain control at a local level and it is backers like you who can make that possible.

Janet Barnes, my assistant, will contact you Monday, (I'll be in California trying to close another supply agreement) to try to confirm your attendance.

Yours truly,

Joe Smith

Joe Smith

ability to change is best demonstrated by documenting your history and strategy in the marketplace.

By the time the readers have finished the product and marketing sections of your plan, they will form their own opinions. In your covering letter and/or executive summary, you should have a simple message: "Our company has a good product and we know how to market it."

Your plan must be well written, clear, and concise. Here are ten basic rules for writing your business plan:

(a) Develop the outline of your foundation modules by categorizing and sub-categorizing the main elements into no more than three levels.

(b) Make sure that there is continuity within the three levels so that the degree of scope and importance is set by heading and subheading levels.

(c) Subheadings should have a logical sequence or priority of importance. Clearly point out the ascending or descending importance of specific issues in your subheadings.

(d) Reinforce your personal opinions and judgments with quotations from objective sources where possible. Do not be afraid to use a philosopher or other writer's quotation. Two or three well-articulated points throughout the plan are enough, however. Do not overdo it and do not plagiarize.

(e) Use footnotes to clarify assumptions or numerical data, especially in financial packages.

(f) Have a clean presentation format with enough white space to allow the reader room for margin notations.

(g) Although the product and marketing sections are largely descriptive, the mathematical emphasis of the financial section demands an orderly sequence of facts and justifications. Discuss balance sheet assets by referring to the latest available balance sheet as it appears in an appendix to the plan. Expand on revenue and expense accounts where necessary in the sequence they appear on the income statement and pro forma projections.

(h) Avoid the overuse of vague qualifiers like "fairly," "some," or "occasionally." Minimize use of technical terms that will be unfamiliar to the reader, but do not sacrifice precision to achieve this. Edit your work to eliminate unnecessary jargon, excessive adjectives, and ambiguous pronouns.

(i) Use comparative data to your advantage. Concise tables or sentences that deal with alternate product traits, market niches, financial implications, or historic precedents can be very effective. Likewise, documentation that contrasts the net effect of two seemingly similar actions can be useful.

(j) Convey a sense of emotion with one or two key statements. Regardless of the fact that business plans are supposed to be objective presentations, a total lack of passion makes your presentation mechanical. All analysts stress the importance of people and team spirit. Direct statements that emphasize a strong level of commitment are important.

Many of the above guidelines are exemplified in the sample business plan in Appendix 1. Style, however, is a personal thing, normally developed by professional writers over a period of time through trial and error, specific training, and, often, an innate talent. If you feel uncomfortable with writing or restricted by time demands, engage a writer and manage the process as you would any other element of your business.

2. Hiring a business plan writer

If you choose to hire an outsider to write your business plan, your first major decision centers on the desired level of your involvement. Do you want an experienced business professional who can actually critique the content of the plan as he or she prepares it? Will you settle for a clever, articulate writer who understands little about your business? While the latter is easier to find, the former may add a valuable perspective. Interview both types of writers before making your choice.

Do some research before you make a decision. First, review their previous work. Ask for samples of similar work and check references. Were reports completed on time and the presentation effective? Was content cohesive and coherent?

Next, arrange for the candidates to have a brief tour of your business; evaluate the quality of questions asked and the ability to listen. Steer away from people who want to talk about themselves; look for a person who concentrates on understanding the business.

When you have narrowed it down, ask your leading candidates to prepare a brief proposal including schedule, cost, and the required accessibility to you and key staff. The quality of that proposal will provide a sound indicator of their abilities to fill your needs.

c. PACKAGING AND PRESENTATION

The business plan should be simple, neat, and compact. It should be double spaced on 8" x 11" paper, typed on one side, and bound so that it can open flat. Coil binding or the flexible perfect binding methods are best.

The cover should show the name of the company and identify the nature of the document.

The title page should include the name of the company contact with the address and telephone number and, if possible, a removable business card.

In many cases, a good color photo of the product or management team is well worth the cost. Using a photo is particularly relevant where the investor has few terms of product reference. On the other hand, everybody knows what a building looks like. Unless location and architecture are a critical part of your business, do not include a photo of the building as your introductory highlight. Computer-generated graphics and tables are fine if used in moderation.

Packaging must take the expected presentation method into account. Ideally, the document is strictly an introduction to be followed by a full presentation from management. If this is improbable, seriously consider a video accompaniment (see section **d.** following). When you do get to the actual presentation, at least two key management people, in addition to the CEO, should attend, and department heads should be available for input as needed. Employee interaction should be courteous and professional, ideally spiced with a sense of camaraderie.

Likely, a first formal meeting will not be at your facility so a tour is out of the question. Do provide a demonstration of your product or technology either through a portable sample or a video. Slide shows are fine for non-dynamic products but tend to suggest a lack of sophistication.

All principles of good sales techniques apply to the corporate presentation. Let your belief in the company and its people shine through.

d. TODAY'S MOST EFFECTIVE SUPPORT TOOLS

1. Spreadsheet programs

Both the software and the accounting professional are well versed in spreadsheet management. It is cost-effective and a necessary item for all companies. Any company with at least five employees should be able to handle word processing, desktop publishing, and spreadsheet programing.

2. Desktop publishing

Desktop publishing (DTP) is the natural extension of word processing. It allows for the creation and integration of computer-generated graphics into full-page formats and the manipulation of all data according to your desire.

DTP differs in scope from the accounting and spreadsheet software. Its visual emphasis demands more sophisticated input/output devices and the software involved is far more extensive.

It was a phenomenon that seemed to occur just yesteryear. When page composition software (i.e., Pagemaker, Quark), the laser printer, and Macintosh computer operating systems burst onto the scene, the world of lithography changed forever. Today five-year-olds are doing it. Peripheral devices like scanners and CD read/write units cost 10% of what they did only a few years ago. Basic printing options are affordable to have in-house, while more sophisticaed print jobs can be produced by service bureaus.

An emerging element of DTP is the growing ability to transmit in-house documents over the Internet. Using print-on-demand services that are springing up everywhere, a company can transmit DTP files to endless different cities and generate new perfect-bound product manuals as needed by local satellite offices.

3. The emerging world of DVD

What was once the realm of the instruction video or corporate PR video has fast given way to DVD technology in which the fundamental world of visual imaging is now combined with the wonders of computer-generated special effects and quality sound tracks. It is reasonable to assume that in the immediate future, DVD will become the primary means of passing on all information that is deemed too slow to move through cyberspace via high-speed lines. The passing of CD read/write was marked the day Hewlett-Packard announced that all further development emphasis was aimed at DVD-RW devices.

Like all technology, DVD's life span is subject to tomorrow's innovation but it does appear to have the broad-based backing and momentum to establish itself for an extended period similar to the life span of the CD.

4. The corporate Web page

Software improvements to support Web site design have been substantial in the last few years, and the relative ease with which companies can create a Web site presence makes this step almost mandatory in modern business.

The real issue for most companies, however, is the extent of effort put into generating customer usage of the site. This is discussed to some extent in the sidebar in chapter 10, titled "The Internet and Your Business," but is really a subject you should educate yourself about in some detail.

5. The sales contract

Of the numerous forms that exist in most businesses, I consider the quality of the corporate sales agreement the most important in the company. Terms of payment are critical to all non-cash businesses and a document that outlines the responsibilities of buyer and seller helps minimize future problems. Readers of your business plan can gain positive insight into your operation by scanning your sales contract. For this reason, including your sales contract form can act as a good support tool to advance any investment proposition.

Sample #3 shows both sides of a single-page document that defines the basic agreement, secures the signature of the customer, clarifies terms of payment, and meets all the legal requirements of contract law. It is not cumbersome and allows adequate flexibility to meet all of the company's needs. A well-conceived standard agreement exemplifies sound management and professionalism.

6. Internet-available services that can help your business

The range of support tools and services that grows daily on the Internet is not to be ignored. One of the most straightforward and most useful to any business hoping to sell directly to international customers is a secure banking service that allows sales and revenue collection in multiple currencies.

In Canada, for instance, it is impossible for a business to make credit card payment deposits in US dollars on the Internet. A service that collects all credit card payments in your currency of choice and passes no credit card information to internal staff negates the possibility of your company being exposed to misuse of credit card information. It also assures you of rapid repayment and deposit of monies into your bank accounts in the currency of choice.

Various Internet services are available in the fields of travel reservations, shipping options, and support software from international shipping companies, and technical databases emerge every day. Companies that stay in touch with new options and bring new efficiences to their businesses will gain a competitive edge.

SAMPLE #3
SALES AGREEMENT

Woodpecker®
Hardwood Floors (1987) Ltd.
Unit 109, 11511 Bridgeport Road, Richmond, B.C., Canada V6X 1T4
Phone (604) 270-0314

Date ________ Cust. Order # ________ Contract # ________

Sold to ________ Phone # ________

Address ________ Postal Code ________

Job Address ________ Phone # ________

We hereby agree to perform the following work in accordance with the specifications and subject to the terms and conditions set forth below and on the reverse hereof:

☐ Supply ☐ Install ☐ Sand & Finish ☐ Stain ☐ Other ________

Type of Floor ________

Grade ________ Size ________ Colour ________ Colour Stain ________

Type of Finish: ☐ Watco (Oil Finish) ☐ Urethane Oil Finish ☐ Gloss ☐ Matte
☐ Water Based Finish ☐ 2 Component Lacquer Finish ☐ Silk-Matte
☐ Glitsa Finish ☐ Other ________

THE FLOOR FINISH MUST BE JUDGED AS A SURFACE ONE WALKS UPON AND CAN NOT BE COMPARED TO FINISHES ON FURNITURE. YOU HAVE BEEN CHARGED IN ACCORDANCE WITH THIS PREMISE.

Remove, Replace or Dispose: ☐ Carpet ☐ Furnishings ☐ Appliances ☐ Mouldings ☐ Other ________

Mouldings: ☐ Supply ☐ Install ☐ Finish Type ________ L/F ________

Treads & Risers: ☐ Supply ☐ Install ☐ Finish L/F ________

☐ Cutting Doors ☐ Re-Install Doors ☐ Remove/Replace Toilet

Areas to be Done ________

Special Instructions ________

This contract is subject to a down payment of $ ________. Balance is net cash upon completion of the job. Any unpaid balance shall bear interest at 2% per month from date of first invoice. This contract is bound by provisions printed on the reverse of this sheet. Unless otherwise specified, contract does NOT include supplying, installing or repairing sub-floor, threshholds or mouldings.

TOTAL CONTRACT PRICE: $________

THIS PROPOSAL AND ALL CONDITIONS CONTAINED THEREIN ARE ACCEPTED. IT IS UNDERSTOOD THAT THIS CONTRACT INCORPORATES BOTH SIDES OF THIS SHEET.

Buyer per ________ Title________ Date ________

Sales Representative ________ Date ________

GUARANTEE

I________ principle of________

the customer herein, in consideration of the acceptance of the payment to me of $1.00 and other good and valuable consideration (the receipt and sufficiency of which is hereby acknowledged) hereby personally guarantee the payment of the above order to Woodpecker Hardwood Floors (1987) Ltd. X________

PRINT NAME

SAMPLE #3
Continued (Back)

TERMS & CONDITIONS

WOODPECKER HARDWOOD FLOORS (1987) LTD. (WHF) guarantees all materials supplied under this contract to be as specified, and to meet or exceed standards of the trade, the Canadian Lumbermen's Association and the National Oak Flooring Manufacturers Association or Maple Flooring Manufacturers Association, and to be free of original defects in material and workmanship for a period of one year from the date of completion of the work specified in this contract. During said one year, Woodpecker Hardwood Floors, Ltd. will remedy or replace any defective part of work specified in the contract at no additional cost to customer, according to the following terms and conditions:

1. This warranty does not apply to any work or materials not provided by WHF
2. This warranty does not apply to any damages caused by factors beyond the control of WHF, such as:
   - latent defects in subfloors, old floors or other materials or work not supplied by WHF;
   - improper maintenance, usual or unusual wear;
   - improper moisture, temperature or ventilation (which causes swelling, buckling, cupping or shrinkage) or insect infestation.
3. WHF shall only be obligated under this warranty for defects which are discovered within one year from date of completion of the work and only if given written notice at address on the reverse hereof of such defect within 13 months of said date of completion.
4. Upon receipt of written notice, WHF shall be allowed 30 days from date of receipt for the purpose of inspecting the premises.
5. WHF shall have sole option of repairing the defect, replacing any material, correcting any work found to be defective, or refunding to customer the contract price paid.
6. The maximum limit of liability of WHF under this warranty shall be the amount actually paid by the customer to WHF under the terms and conditions of their contract.
7. There are no warranties expressed or implied with respect to the labour and materials furnished by WHF except as specifically set forth herein, and no representation or warranty made by any sales or other representative of WHF concerning fitness for a particular purpose or any other warranty, expressed or implied, which is not specifically set forth herein shall be binding upon WHF.
8. WHF assumes no liability for cancellation of non-completion of job due to causes beyond the control of WHF including acts of God, labour disputes or material shortages.
9. WHF assumes no responsibility for imperfections in sub-floor and does not guarantee flooring against cupping, buckling and shrinkage as hardwood flooring expands and contracts with changes in atmospheric moisture levels.

CUSTOMER agrees to:

1. Keep job free from any obstructions or conflicts that would tend to interfere with the performance or work of WHF.
2. Provide WHF exclusive access to areas covered by this contract during the performance of work specified in this contract, and areas to be covered are to be cleared of other workers, equipment, materials, and drapes. Carpet, furniture, and appliances to be cleared by customer unless otherwise specified in this contract. Carpet includes pad and tackstrip and staples.
3. Supply WHF with adequate electric power (220 volts) to operate equipment on the job.
4. Protect flooring from damage by dampness, extreme heat or cold, or strong sunlight. Building must be closed in, heat must be turned on one week prior to delivery of flooring and maintained at 16C (65F) for the duration of work regardless of the season.
5. Carry adequate fire, vandalism and other necessary insurance.

BOTH PARTIES AGREE:

1. This proposal, when signed by both parties, becomes a contract binding on both parties.
2. In the event any legal process is employed to enforce any terms of this agreement, the prevailing party shall be entitled to legal fees, court costs and interest.
3. WHF shall not be responsible for noise and dust created by floor installation equipment.
4. Flooring should be installed at least one week before sanding and finishing, and before any carpets are laid.
5. In the event work must be stopped while job is in progress due to changes by customer or unforeseen defects such as dry rot, insect infestation, etc.), the customer will pay for additional labour time incurred. If the situation can be remedied on the job by the installer, he will do so with customer's consent and additional costs will be charged by WHF.
6. This agreement is subject to credit approval by WHF. Neither party is liable for delay or cancellation due to causes beyond their control, but any other cancellation is subject to a charge of 10% for Liquidated Damages.
7. WHF is not liable for any consequential or incidental damage, or for any loss resulting form installation of materials supplied by WHF.

e. WHO SEES THE BUSINESS PLAN?

If you have expectations for the company that you will share with your banker, then share them with your management team. Individual salaries and employment terms are not normally presented in business plans and this negates the only logical reason for excluding managers from total accessibility to the plan.

It has always amazed me when executives develop a business strategy and are then reluctant to share it with their key personnel. How can you involve people in your parade if they do not know what they are marching for? Why are some businesspeople afraid to tell employees that they are there to make a profit? Isn't the business plan the way to start?

On the other hand, you don't want to provide an indiscriminate supply of uncontrolled copies of your plan. Stamp your plan "confidential," document the number of copies in circulation, and restrict all copying where possible. If you send your business plan to funding sources, request its return at the appropriate time.

There are certain people that you do not want to see the plan — your competition for instance. If your plan is based on exclusive information, you will want to avoid triggering alternate investment proposals from opportunistic promoters who use your documentation to enter the market.

I vividly recall assisting a company who was seeking seed capital to develop a major new tourist service. Directed to a well-known stock promoter, we were encouraged to provide extensive technical literature to verify the design feasibility and certification standards for a unique water recreation vehicle. After doing our own investigation of the audience (too late, mind you, and before I knew what I know now!), we decided to avoid further involvement with this questionable character. Six months later this opportunist had his own company, his own technical package remarkably similar to the one presented by my client, and a slick promotion package extracted largely from a misplaced copy of our business plan.

If you are using a third party to assist in funding and they will have liberty to distribute your plan, insist that you receive precise information on who sees it.

10
COMMON MISCONCEPTIONS IN BUSINESS PLANNING

Over the years, I have polled advisers to small business start-ups as well as successful businesspeople, and I have formed my own opinions on the most common misconceptions of new entrepreneurs. Here is a summary of the oversights, misinterpretations, and naive expectations that can lead to disappointment. It is better that you know the truth now.

a. THE REAL COST OF MONEY

Why should anyone in his or her right mind provide you an unsecured loan at "prime plus 2%" to enter an unproven business in an unproven market with an unproven management team? About half the fund seekers in the business world enter their project thinking this kind of money is available. When the banks and venture capitalists politely reject their requests, some of these "businesspeople" then turn to friends and relatives to offer them the same deal. If real investors say no thanks, then the next step is to play on the emotions of loved ones and encourage them to make a bad business decision.

A high percentage of start-ups are funded by people who know and believe in the entrepreneur. If you value your friendships in life, be very careful about mixing them with money. Business losses are one thing: alienating loved ones is a much larger burden to bear. If you must use the capital of friends and relatives, at least offer them rewards compatible with the risk they assume.

If government or blue chip corporate bonds yield the investor 5% to 7%, what must your deal pay to attract those investment dollars? While you are optimistic about your chances, statistics are against you. Investment bankers who back some of the most sophisticated new technologies long after the seed capital start-up phase still want a 30% return on investment to compensate for perceived risk. Those providing seed capital deserve even higher returns.

As a simple guideline for new or revised business plans of companies that require a financial infusion, you will have to provide the investors a reasonable possibility of getting their money back within two years and earning 40% to 50% of their original investment thereafter.

My suggestion is simple. If you use friendly money, deal with the two key issues up front. First, offer a two-phase reward system. If the venture projects a longer payback period than three years, acknowledge this and provide some form of extended reward if payback is delayed beyond a certain point.

Second, discuss the possibility of failure up front. Be realistic and explore how failure would affect your relationship. Don't put your parents' retirement fund into a neighborhood auto repair shop unless everybody knows that statistically half of such attempts leave everyone broke within two years.

b. REDUCING THE COST OF MONEY AND THE AMOUNT NEEDED

Once you come to grips with the cost of money and deal with the moral question of paying less to friends and relatives, you may have a pleasant surprise. There are ways to reduce the cost of money and ways to reduce the amount of money needed.

1. Investment tax credits and municipal bonds

Cities, states, and provinces in the United States and Canada share a strong desire for economic growth and they have found ways to help small businesses get a foothold. There are local and regional tax reduction programs for investors of small business. Usually there are restrictions tied to the nature of the business and the benefactor is intended to be the private investor.

You should explore the possibilities in your locale and clearly understand the guidelines. Often incentives are restricted based on job creation in the manufacturing and development sectors. Two examples can illustrate how these programs reduce the cost of money for business planners.

Some jurisdictions have legislated into existence a class of company called Venture Capital Corporations (VCCs). Investors use this vehicle to fund new business ventures and receive an immediate tax credit based on the size of their investment. That tax credit allows the investor to deduct up to 30%, for example, of total cash investment as a credit against taxes payable. The benefit to the small business is obvious. As an investment, they offer an immediate reward and the direct cost of money is reduced substantially. If an investor advanced $100,000 to get a $30,000 tax credit and reduced his or her tax bill accordingly, he or she has a net exposure of $70,000. Rather than expect a $100,000 payback and $40,000 to $50,000 a year thereafter, he or she need see only $70,000 in two years and $35,000 thereafter.

Municipal bonds are also restricted in their use and work only with the full cooperation of local government. In the early 1980s, the city of Corpus Christi, Texas, was anxious to promote tourist growth along the local waterfront and wanted to encourage hotel expansion to complement their new convention center. Because municipal bonds are tax free to the investor, the city was willing to issue such bonds and transfer the funds to private enterprise to build hotels. This technique would cut the cost of traditional mortgage money almost in half.

Government programs are usually plagued by red tape, but they are well worth investigating. It may even be worth broadening your search for an operating site to a locale that offers such a possibility. Government competition for regional economic growth is a big thing these days and tax concessions are common. Keep an open mind.

2. Supplier financing

Perhaps part of your planned business expenditure calls for a major investment in inventory or capital equipment. Assume for the moment that the prime supplier has a gross profit margin of 60% on the goods they supply you. In other words, if they ship you $100,000 worth of product, their actual direct cost of components was $40,000. They actually had to lay out $40,000 more cash to fill your order than they would have if you never appeared at their door. Therefore, their true exposure is only $40,000. Naturally, you will have trouble convincing any major supplier to invest $40,000 with you based on gaining investment recognition for direct costs only. Still, these things are a matter of perception and its a great place to start — especially if the supplier wants to break into a new market.

Dave Dent had a business plan to open a new body and paint shop in the fast-growing suburbs north of Atlanta, Georgia. Initially, his first draft allocated the need for $50,000 for spray-painting booths critical to his operational concept. After the cold shoulder from local banks, he sought to reduce his actual cash requirement. Ninety percent of the certified paint booths in Georgia came from DV Corp, the southeast's largest supplier. When Dave asked for a purchase deal at 40% down with the remainder in two years at 15% interest, the local distributor laughed at him.

Dave called his brother in Cleveland to seek out other northern suppliers. Two weeks later, with an adapted plan, he had secured a commitment for three booths from an aggressive young company anxious to move into southern markets. His revised business plan called for his shop to act as the major demonstration site for all southwest distribution, and Dave was given sales agency status. The first three booths were supplied COD at 40% of retail, and additional promotion and maintenance support was guaranteed by the manufacturer. By finding the right supplier and recognizing a mutual business interest, Dave Dent reduced his investment need by $30,000 and had an unforeseen associate keenly interested in the success of his business.

If you do get into bed with a major supplier, it is in your best interest to minimize long-term commitment. There should be an out clause in any supply agreement. You cannot get three years into your business and have commitments to a supplier to buy stock at an uncompetitive price with no recourse to go elsewhere.

There are many variations of this transaction, but the basic premise is always the same. Suppliers need customers and any deal that reduces net cash outlay and/or offers a chance at extra reward is worth considering. It is a marriage of financial convenience. The only real rule in such matters is the need for mutual commitment. Each party must have some financial exposure that assures their direct interest in project success.

c. REDUCING DIRECT STAFF COSTS

1. Sweat equity

Many of the great corporate empires of today owe their existence to the greatest survival compromise in the history of business. During the depression, fortunes were lost but many future fortunes were made. Some creative business leaders rejected defeat and rallied their employees to commit to joint survival.

In Walkerville, Ontario, a small Canadian community across the river from Detroit, things were tough in the 1930s. The major employer, Hiram Walker (now a world-renowned distiller), was up against the ropes and only the president's resolve to survive kept things afloat. He made a proposal to all employees. "Work for stock and the few pennies that will feed your family. Believe in this company and we will all win."

Through the 1950s and early 1960s, janitors and executives alike retired as millionaires, thanks to their acceptance of "sweat equity."

The most invigorating business environment in existence is the one where employees have a piece of the action. If your business plan demands a $250,000 payroll over the next year, consider the following:

(a) About $75,000 of the $250,000 will go for income tax and not stay with the employee.

(b) Employee turnover is dramatically lower in companies with equity participation.

(c) Team commitment to common business objectives forms a bonding pattern that lasts for years.

(d) Productivity gains over the life of the relationship can be enormous.

Because tax legislation encourages employee equity, the same net cash benefits apply to employee equity plans as in tax credit investments. The methodology, however, is usually different. You should contact your accountant to review possibilities in your jurisdiction.

2. Using contract help

I believe that retaining non-employees to do specific jobs for fixed fees on guaranteed schedules is preferable, in many instances, to hiring full-time people. Certainly, there is an obvious need for full-time employees in many positions. But many companies had to rethink their hiring policies after the recession of the early 1980s, and experienced businesses who found themselves victimized by corporate obesity now strive to say lean if not mean.

Both at the cost-projection stage and in practice, the use of contract labor can serve you well. Before you agree to hire a new permanent person, look closely at the job mandate, its duration, the ability of the candidates to grow with your needs, and the dynamics of the job description. Even if you do foresee long-term needs, get to know potential employees by retaining them on a project basis. Performance-oriented people are growing more inclined to work this way.

d. THE EASE-OF-ENTRY PROBLEM

Most business planners totally ignore the ease-of-entry problem and its implications. They explain how simple and low-risk their venture is and how much money it will make. They write a summary that says "This is so easy that anybody could do it, and if you invest in me I'll make you a million dollars." If it is that easy, then, indeed, anyone can and will do it.

Think for a minute about the 1980s' VCR phenomenon. This home entertainment device created an exciting, new small business opportunity. A few pioneers jumped at the chance and opened neighborhood rental centers. Some were add-ons to existing businesses, but many were stand-alone operations that quickly found themselves in trouble as supply came to exceed demand. Deeper pockets entered the supply side of a lucrative market and provided 24-hour shops in high-traffic, easy-access sites. Corner markets got into the act, as did gas stations and the supermarkets. Ease of entry killed a thousand small business investors that were sure they had a winner.

If you are seeking professional financing, it is absolutely critical to have some element of your business that foils ease of entry. It can be patents, copyrights, secret codes, proprietary software, exclusive rights, or unique real estate — otherwise you have a major hill to climb.

e. BUSINESSES THAT TRAIN THEIR COMPETITION

Wise investors do not like the idea of a business with high front-end staff training costs. Worse are the industries that actually develop their own competition.

There are exceptions. Many say that IBM trained the entire computer industry during the 1960s and 1970s and developed just enough competition to save them from anti-trust penalties. While any Macintosh fan will condemn this exaggeration, the success of IBM proves that you can still succeed even if you train a lot of people who leave your company.

The real problem lies in plans for small-scale businesses that assume a regular buildup of business from the steady growth of loyal staff. Beauty salons are notorious for facing this problem. You hire a stylist recently relocated from another city. Eighteen months later the employee rents a hole in the wall, hangs out a shingle, and takes a good percentage of your regular clients down the street. It's a real problem, and smart investors know it, so the business planner must respond with a policy like the following: "To face our most serious industry problem, we have devised a unique shared-revenue escalation program for our most productive senior stylists, a program we are confident will aid our growth plan and reduce staff turnover."

Few businesses can fully eliminate the possibility of training future competition. Technology and product development companies, however, should always have employees sign formal secrecy commitments that surrender rights to any intellectual properties created while they are an employee. This policy will heighten the investor respect for your research efforts.

THE INTERNET AND YOUR BUSINESS

I earlier alluded to Web pages and the ease-of-entry problem of the Internet. Probably the most unique aspect of the Internet is the electronic facade that can be presented to the world. The ingenuity, energy, and time that have gone into creating distinct Web sites are phenomenal. Corporate America has been left in the dust by teenagers, artisans, and groovy grannies from coast to coast. It truly is the people's medium. This doesn't mean that a whole range of businesses haven't thrived while creating links to the Internet. But making money on the Net itself is a different ball game.

While the Internet itself has exploded into an endless source of information and access to anything that can be digitized, it still remains a challenge to the individual business. Can it be a cost-effective management or marketing tool or will your business join the legions who have piddled away much of the profit made in their traditional business on their journey into cyberspace? The temptations of the Internet are many because the potential seems infinite and the world of dot.com remains anxious to lure you in their direction.

Business planners need to look at four distinct aspects of the Internet. Most of the hype around the Internet focuses on consumer marketing, and that is a valid consideration. However, for many businesses, the effective harnessing of this venue may relate more to using it as a corporate intranet or providing a database that allows various business associates to rapidly access information you can provide. Other uses may include a restricted but readily available corporate "bulletin board" that allows sales reps or other personnel to access new internal information anywhere, anytime. Finally, business must recognize that the Internet is the most exciting and potentially valuable new source of accessible information since the creation of the public library.

While it is beyond the scope of this book to dig deeply into Internet usage, brief answers to four questions may help guide you in the planning process.

1. **What are the critical elements of consumer marketing on the Internet?**

For e-commerce to succeed, any product or service promoted on the Internet must first meet the same standards of excellence required to succeed in traditional business. Second, the process of getting the purchased item to the consumer must be carefully analyzed and the handling costs minimized. Books are a classic example in that it would be far more cost effective if books were sent directly to consumers from the printers rather than from printers to publisher warehouses, to online bookseller warehouses, and finally to the consumer.

Site design has emerged with new tools and techniques available to the Webmaster, but the success rate remains extremely low. Keep it simple, neat, and inviting. Ask what the consumer needs to know to make the "buy" decision and provide it.

Probably the most challenging element of consumer marketing is finding a way to attract traffic. All search engines use distinct criteria to prioritize sites on search lists. New information is continually written on this subject and endless services exist to help get you to page one. It is my belief that as the entire system gets more sophisticated, small business stands to gain by becoming more precise in their description of service rather than generating "hits" due to general descriptions that place them in the haystack of listings a hundred pages deep on some consumer search.

2. **What distinguishes a non-consumer site from a consumer-oriented site?**

Many businesses are changing the need for hardcopy user manuals, product catalogues, tariff sheets, and other information files that are subject to alteration and readily accessible to educated parties who need the information. In planning elements of how a business can budget costs and design information sources, the establishment of a component of your Web site that is only accessible by code to qualified users can provide tremendous savings in the long run.

The key to success here is education. It must be demonstrated and confirmed by your customer that using the Internet to access valuable information you provide is a satisfactory experience.

3. **How can an "electronic bulletin board" work for the small company?**

It makes no sense to create an e-board if you have a three-employee company in constant contact. If you have people in four locations and two traveling salespeople who rarely see each other, then it is a good idea to have a specific place where all who need to know can stay in touch with corporate happenings by accessing the e-board. The process is simple in that a component of the corporate Web site is partitioned with no direct means of accessing it. Qualified employees are simply provided an extension code that they can add to the Web site address to access the e-board. Communication will always be key to business success, and this is a cheap new way to communicate as an add-on to e-mail.

4. **How is the Internet best used as a source of information?**

This is a very difficult question to answer in that there are no right and wrong answers other than to suggest some self-discipline in staying focussed. Certainly, information gathering about competition is easier, at least for those progressive enough to have some Web site presence.

Simple advice here is for the business planner who still resists the lure of the Net to try to devote a couple of hours per week to exploring information sources and really discover the scope of information that may help his or her businesses.

f. CAPITAL-INTENSIVE BUSINESSES WITHOUT LIQUIDATION POTENTIAL

I sometimes wonder how the first tourist submarine was ever built. Think about it. An entrepreneur brings in a picture and a business plan and needs $2.5 million to build a prototype. What can you recoup if it doesn't work?

This was one of the biggest challenges faced by company president, Dennis Hurd of Sub Aquatics Corporation as the company developed its business plan. Fortunately, in this case, their unique potential offset this serious roadblock to success and they are now a world leader in tourist submersibles.

There are some front-end compromises that may constitute the difference between success and failure. While I have never actually seen a company do this, if you need money to demonstrate a prototype or distribution concept, you might use the following technique.

Calculate the liquidation value of components if it fails. I am not suggesting that you compromise your likelihood of success by planning for failure. I am suggesting that taking the time to evaluate the aftermarket for components provides a means of diminishing perceived risk if the investor is given a first charge against capital-intensive assets. If you leave it totally to the money sources to do this, they may paint a dimmer picture without your input and, therefore, overstate their exposure.

g. SORTING THE FADS FROM THE TRENDS

What are fads and what are permanent changes in the North American psyche? It's not always easy to know. Labeled T-shirts outlived the fad handle but leg warmers didn't. Skateboards are here for a long time. Michael Jackson gloves will die in closets, as did a lot of Davy Crockett hats.

Fads are more commonly associated with the young and are destined to live a short intense life before succumbing to the next phenomena. Fads and trends can, however, be linked. The music industry is an ongoing treadmill of one-hit wonders or fads, while the popularity of music styles over the past 50 years is more defined by trends.

For the business planner trying to distinguish between fad and trend, demographics can no doubt play a role. Consumer tastes do relate to age and circumstance. Consider "G-Force" and the move to Grey Power in the new millennium. G-Force is symbolized by the growing appeal of golf, gardening, and gambling — all well-documented growth pastimes among the early boomer retirees. Each activity occupies leisure time and provides satisfaction in one form or another to the participant.

Trends are to a degree predictable. Fads often defy logic or originate from a mindset that pollsters and market researchers have yet to tap into. I'm not sure if there are any bankers that a decade ago would have backed a body-piercing salon. On the other hand, lots of numbers exist to show that a growing number of businessmen in their fifties will flock to specialty medical clinics for all-inclusive, full-service personal checkups they used to reserve for their sports cars.

In business planning, it is almost impossible to articulate the logic of responding to a fad. While lots of money can be made catering to either short- or intermediate-term demands in a niche market, the window of opportunity is usually small enough that it requires gut instinct and a predator instinct to succeed. Business planners don't start fads. The pet rock came out of a basement, not a boardroom.

h. REAL ESTATE AND YOUR BUSINESS PLAN

Some business planners have trouble dealing with real estate in the planning phase. I give full marks to the planner who tries to justify a self-owned business site within three years of starting up and allocates cash accordingly. Probably half of the small businesses that survive five years and have their own facility end up making more money selling their land than they do selling their business.

i. SUPPLIER DEPENDENCE

Supplier dependence is different than supplier financing. A supplier who finances you has a vested interest in your survival. But you can imagine the panic at an interactive computer system company when they found that a key system component was being discontinued. Twenty technical experts had developed a simulation system around a circuit board they assumed would always be available. As technology improved, the board became obsolete and the manufacturer no longer produced them. To the computer company, $7 million of product development was suddenly at risk. Although the matter was resolved, the simulator was delayed for weeks because of a $100 circuit board.

One of the major problems of high-tech planning is the dynamics of progress. Products are being rendered obsolete before they ever reach the marketplace. Suppliers come and go, and a lack of industry uniform standards sends equipment to the junk pile.

j. LACK OF IDENTITY

Who are you and where do you come from? Who stands behind you and what companies are you associated with? Are there familiar names on your customer list? Household names help sell business plans and at least one such identity is critical. If you have an agreement to supply paper goods to McDonald's, your business plan will be well received. If the contract is with Nickel Toilets of America, there may be less enthusiasm.

Anybody can be a name dropper. Sometimes you just can't print it. I have never seen a town without a celebrity ready to sell his or her name. There are big names and falling stars available for every budget.

If you're in the golf business, you might get Arnold Palmer or Jack Nicklaus for $250,000 up front or the local hero for $5,000 a year. Entertainers will sing your song and politicians will kiss your babies. Right or wrong, attaching a recognizable image to your company can help you in both the marketplace and the investor boardroom.

k. NATIONAL DISTRIBUTION

Business planners are often naive about distribution strategy and target marketing. There are six major distribution regions in the United States and four in Canada. Depending on the business, traditional channels have emerged that might have little similarity between regions. It can be narrow-minded for a manufacturer to insist on the same policy across the continent in most product lines. A business plan that makes unfounded distribution statements is vulnerable to immediate criticism.

11
CONCLUSION

a. THE VIRTUES OF INNOVATION

Any discussion of the craft of preparing a successful business plan would be incomplete without raising the critical contribution to success attributable to a single human trait: the capacity to innovate.

There was never a team that did not benefit from the spirit and imagination of an innovative quarterback. And in a time of rapid technological change and the ever-accelerated dynamics of today's business arena, the ability to innovate often separates the survivors from the condemned.

Innovation is not to be confused with invention. It is usually more a case of adaptation than creation, and it is a talent that can be learned. The purpose of this section is simply to give you some of my thoughts on the subject and spur you to pursue readings and explore methods that will make you more innovative. Think of it as aerobics for the mind.

Being innovative involves four key elements:

(a) a capacity to quickly analyze or absorb the current state of things,

(b) a further capacity to isolate the elements critical to adapting the status quo to the desired state,

(c) the imagination to conjure up viable scenarios to achieve the desired state, and

(d) the management skills to harness specific resources and pursue the goal.

Research suggests that there are specific characteristics commonly associated with innovative people. One such trait is an entrepreneur's ability to listen to team input and help develop creative group thoughts. More often the traits of the successful innovator relate to personal regimen. Dr. Denis Waitley, in his book *Winning the Innovation Game,* painted innovative people as being stubborn, intuitive, realistic, opportunistic, and resourceful. The subjects he studied approached daily events with an open mind and exercised vision when presented with a specific dilemma. They were able to anticipate the course of events and they almost automatically weighed both the risk and reward of any specific course of action. In the immortal words of Muhammad Ali, they had learned both "to float like a butterfly and sting like a bee."

Instilling an innovative mindset in a group environment is a true challenge. How often have you sat in a group of seasoned veterans where a common response to solution seekers is, "We tried that already." The prejudice of experience is often one of the great dampers in a forum of peers. Be it ego or sincere belief, an amazing percentage of people automatically reject any idea that seems similar on the surface to some past failure. They feel that because a course of action taken to resolve a past business challenge failed in a given time and place, it should be denied further consideration under any circumstance.

Disciples of innovation reject such thought. Waitley quotes David Packard of Hewlett Packard in his challenge to corporate engineers. "Make a technical contribution. Innovate, don't emulate." This may apply to Packard's task at hand, but for many businesses a better motto may be a variation on an old Kenny Rogers' song: "Know when to emulate; know when to innovate." And innovation is not limited to product engineering. In fact, innovative marketing programs are often more relevant in small business or home-based businesses that are service oriented.

Take for example the Internet, where many companies are developing their Web sites with little grasp of what they are trying to achieve. As the massive number of sites grows exponentially with each passing month, most of the site development effort has gone into esthetics and user-friendly site architecture to allow site visitors to explore. Probably the most innovative work is being done behind the scenes. Anybody who has surfed the Internet knows that a search request using two or three key words can stack thousands of options. All the major search engines have their unique software criteria for stacking and setting priority. No matter how pretty your site is, few will find it unless an innovative approach has been taken to get you near the front of the search engine lists in all categories that might bring you customers. Ultimately, I expect that those companies that succeed using the Internet will need to apply ingenuity both in drawing customers to the site and captivating them once they are there.

b. YOUR BUSINESS PLAN AS A TANGIBLE ASSET

The development of a business plan takes a great deal of time and effort by senior management. That means that it is an expensive proposition to undertake. As mentioned in chapter 1, the major motivation for most companies to commit this time is the pursuit of capital funding. The tragedy in many companies is that, once the funding is complete, they toss the plan aside and devote their collective energy to "management by crisis."

The contrasting attitudes toward business plans was exemplified in an *Inc.* magazine article called "The Best Laid Plans." Scott McNealy, CEO of Sun Microsystems, found the business plan produced by his co-founders obsolete within a year. "You basically throw out all assumptions every three weeks," is his impression of the fast-moving computer industry. His rationale is that their original sales projections doubled and tripled in their first two years, so the plan became obsolete.

Mr. McNealy may have an extraordinary ability to run a hundred-employee business with no written agenda, but he misses a key point. The planning process was a part of the initial success and of apparent value to those around him. Through the life of a company, plans are not intended for the amusement of successful entrepreneurs, they are communications documents to help all managers understand both the goals of the company and the means of reaching them.

Bill Foster, CEO of Stratus Computer Inc., has much more appreciation for this fact. In the same article, he states "The plan was something we took very seriously. Our first year of sales we were behind plan, and we were really concerned; we really pushed hard. If the original plan had a lower goal, we would have achieved less." Foster's appreciation for his business plan has not ebbed with time and success. "I really value this thing. This is probably the most important document I have."

Planning is like most repetitive processes — the more often you do it the more adept you become. *Inc.'s* survey found that venture capitalists truly feel that a business plan provides the ideal vehicle for management to think through its strategies. If this is the case, it logically follows that the repeated updating of the plan provides an ideal forum for strategy reviews.

Much is to be learned from comparing the realities of the past six months or year to your original expectations.

There are very few tangible ways to assess management performance. Using money as the sole criterion rarely satisfies the complexity of most business growth curves. Companies that think of their original founding business plan as a dusty artifact have missed an opportunity to be better at what they do.

Perhaps the tendency to discard past plans is a more significant management problem than many entrepreneurs wish to admit. Hard copy can be embarrassing.

The approach discussed in this book is designed to integrate business planning into the ongoing role of company management and recognize that looking into the future is a challenging task. There is no place for embarrassment once hindsight is at hand. The original business plan can always be a tangible building block.

APPENDIX 1
SAMPLE BUSINESS PLAN

The sample plan shown in this appendix is a compilation of information used by a start-up company intent on raising $150,000 for the initial phase of a two-phase fundraising program to develop a prototype unit and establish production and distribution facilities across North America. In this example, some of the technical information has been left vague at the request of the company.

While this sample covers many of the points discussed in the text, no single business program can respond to all of the issues that the entrepreneur must consider.

ULTRASONIC LIFEGUARD CORPORATION

Executive Summary

Ultrasonic Lifeguard Corporation (ULC) has been formed exclusively to develop, produce, and distribute a product group aimed at the swimming pool security and water safety needs of North America.

The company has identified a specific void in the marketplace and a consumer demand for a technical solution to the nationwide concern about child safety near swimming pools. Principals of the company have interviewed media personnel, insurance industry executives, concerned citizens' groups, legislators, and consumer advocates to establish the range of support for the product concept. Approval has been unanimous.

There are over 3,000 serious immersion accidents and drownings of children under the age of five in residential, public, and hotel swimming pools in North America each year. To date, devices aimed at reducing these tragedies through an alarm system in unguarded pools have been lacking in technical design. ULC feels that their ultrasonic detection system is the solution and preliminary testing shows verification of an accurate means of identifying unintentional immersions of children, pets, and other materials in swimming pools.

ULC's first production model will operate off a low-voltage line and is affixed in a single corner of any square, rectangular, or L-shaped pool. Patent submissions are currently being prepared and both UL listing and CSA approval are expected before we proceed with distribution.

The technical product specification will be completed three months after conclusion of the phase one financing. In parallel, an external product design specialist has been retained to refine the housing design and cosmetic features of the product and its packaging. The entire configuration will displace less than 72 cubic inches and have no negative esthetic effect on the pool area.

ULC's marketing strategy during the next year will emerge in three steps. Initially, test units will be placed in totally controlled environments to develop consumer and institutional endorsements for its technical merit. After three months of testing, a specific city (likely Seattle) will be targeted as the test market center and 50 installations will be completed in interior and outdoor settings. Participation by at least two major hotel chains is expected at this time.

Assuming no technical delays, the product will be unveiled nationally at the annual gatherings of the American Hotel Association and California swimming pool industry trade show early next year.

The company is currently considering two alternate distribution strategies. First, we will undertake to establish our own product identification and a product line for distribution through an agency and wholesale network that supplies the pool maintenance industry. Second, we will consider component supply and/or product assembly for established manufacturers of industry products on an OEM basis.

Future models are expected to tie in to existing home alarm systems and others will eventually run off solar power.

The company has assessed its financial needs and expects to raise money through two development phases and a final entry into full-scale product assembly. The budget for the initial phase is $150,000 pegged for cash disbursement plus an estimated $100,000 of development input to be supplied by the principals.

At this stage the company has not formatted a specific investment structure and is interested in talking with professional investors with the resources to fund both development stages on a conditional basis. The initial commitment of $150,000 would be followed by an additional $250,000 infusion on the proviso that the company achieve its phase one development goals on budget.

Ultrasonic Lifeguard Corporation's management team consists of the three founders who collectively possess the technical and marketing talents and experience to achieve success in this venture. Personal profiles are provided in the body of the report.

The primary goal of this entity is to become a profitable company in its second year of operation and establish industry leadership in the swimming pool market niche known as "immersion surveillance." Our mission is to exercise prudent application of available funding to develop a unique, patent-protected product line and achieve mass distribution to the consumer market. The target retail price of the product is $279 U.S. and the target direct manufacturing cost at break-even levels is $30, based on current component prices.

The Company and Its Product

Ultrasonic Lifeguard Corporation is the proposed name of a new company, to be formed specifically to advance the technology applications which distinguish its prototype design of a unique swimming pool safety device. The company intends to establish an identity as the technology leader in child safety systems around residential swimming pools. Its formation has resulted from the combined efforts of the management group to define a viable means of meeting demand for a product that will protect pool areas from unauthorized and/or accidental entry when the pool is unattended.

Numerous forms of motion and sound detectors have emerged in the past 20 years aimed at solving this problem. However, all have operated within a tolerance range less than ideal for the task at hand. Either their operation is inconsistent across the total pool surface or the alarm sensitivities and indiscriminate trigger systems cause them to rapidly lose credibility with the owner. Most are based on surface or periphery surveillance and can be influenced by such factors as wind, twigs, and even heavy rain.

Other more sophisticated methods are technically plausible but at substantial product cost and installation complexity. The ULC Lifesaver One will operate on the principle of subsurface plane surveillance and will recognize all entry and submersion to the detection depth when the unit is activated. By isolating the sensory process to respond to items that "qualify" as possible child or pet entry into the pool, the system can eliminate the likelihood of false alarms. It is the application of ultrasonic wave technology under the control of a programmed microchip that forms the basis for this invention. Tied in to a low-voltage transformer, the electrical aspects of the product will conform to all industry standards and certification needs.

The swimming pool servicing industry provides an ideal distribution environment for such a product in that an established installation and maintenance infrastructure is well entrenched in most communities. A secondary industry that will also find this an attractive add-on product is the growing home security system business.

A competitive survey of alternate products is currently being completed and will soon be available to interested parties. Preliminary investigation suggests that no suitable product has yet emerged that qualifies for endorsement by the numerous national and state organizations intent on minimizing child drownings in residential pools. Likewise, the insurance industry, anxious to provide incentives for the installation of such safety devices, has yet to applaud a product that meets the functional criteria to make it practical.

The Marketing Plan

Currently, there are in the marketplace two basic types of pool security systems that are popular. Motion detecting, battery-operated systems like the Remington recognize wave action and respond with a built-in alarm or, on more expensive models (about $200 Cdn.), signal a remote alarm in the home. Perimeter systems, on the other hand, use infrared or ultrasonic detectors to recognize penetration of the pool perimeter by humans or animals. These systems require strategic placement of reflectors and can cost up to $500. There is no underwater sonic system currently available according to industry sources.

Industry marketing personnel identify three key factors in determining the likelihood of achieving large volume sales. Ease of installation is the most critical factor for "do-it-yourself" aftermarket installations. Adjustable sensitivities and alarm volumes are important and point-of-sale display packaging is also key.

The main consumer issue of easy installation dictates that the ideal system will be battery operated and the choice of increased product size to accommodate power source is preferable to the need for direct electrical connection. It is recommended that the system be able to monitor battery status and identify the need for a battery change by incorporating a remote receiver.

Distribution channels in the industry tend to take two forms. Some manufacturers use direct sales reps or territorial agents to sell directly to retailers. Others rely totally on distributors who stock and wholesale products within their regions. In Vancouver there are two distributors who both wholesale and retail product and one exclusive wholesaler who looks for a 20% to 25% gross margin on sales. A conversation with John Verschaer, Sales Manager of Aquaform, the largest western Canadian distributor, suggests that a $200 retail unit would be sold by them for $130 to $140 and they would expect to pay $105 to $115 from the manufacturer.

There are two major trade shows worth noting. The National Spa and Pool Show alternates between coasts and will next be held in Florida in November 2002. The CanSpa show is held annually in Toronto at about the same time.

The following steps are required to assure development of a marketable product and reflect upon the ULC strategy for the next six months.

1. The aid of an experienced industry marketer should be enlisted to help establish a product specification.
2. Once the technical specification is set a product design specialist must be recruited to aid in the esthetic design.
3. One or two company managers should attend the Orlando show to assess the competitive environment and provide access to national distributors, manufacturers, and buyers.
4. Market analysis should be targeted at the industry wholesaler and retailer network to identify sales barriers and general impressions of the technology and its merit.
5. Competitive analysis will require a review of all systems in the marketplace, their method of distribution, packaging and pricing, installation process, alarm traits, esthetics, and corporate support.

A major factor supporting the market potential of immersion protection devices is the growing awareness of the child drowning issue. The U.S. Consumer Product Safety Commission in Washington has made the reduction of child drownings a priority project. In sunbelt states like California, Arizona, and Florida, drowning is the leading cause of accidental death for small children. They liken the scope of the problem to child poisoning before enactment of the Poison Prevention Packaging Act of 1970. In conjunction with the National Spa and Pool Institute, the Safety Commission has undertaken to advance pool safety nationwide and has indicated a strong desire to encourage more effective pool alarm systems.

Commission studies reveal that the major problems they face involve:

(a) the impossible task of fully securing a backyard pool with a fence and gate perimeter;

(b) the speed and *silence* with which a submersion and drowning may occur;

(c) that adults are commonly nearby but unaware of the accident when it occurs.

There were 2.2 million in-ground pools in the United States (average cost range $8,300 to $29,700) in 1986 and 2.3 million above-ground pools (average cost range $600 to $3,200). Submersion accidents in these pools had a social economic cost estimated at $450 million to $600 million in 1983. The number of deaths for children under five has grown alarmingly (260 in 1984, 280 in 1985, 330 in 1986).

The commission sponsored testing of four alarm detection systems under restricted disclosure and concluded that "although they generally performed in accordance with the manufacturer's literature, significant problems with false alarms and/or failure to alarm were encountered during testing of each of the devices...the commission staff does not consider the devices tested as capable of providing completely reliable warnings."

This commission has expressed a keen interest in any new sensory technology applications that will reduce child drowning and is currently reviewing the feasibility of alternate technologies.

Marketing Strategy

The company believes that its state-of-the-art technology will quickly make it the industry leader in the field of immersion surveillance. In this role, it will face a major marketing decision regarding licensing of its technology versus exclusive product distribution of its own models.

At this stage, the first priority is to establish in-house commercial product and prove market demand. Only by totally controlling the emergence of the technology can we maximize the corporate potential at this time. However, we will give serious consideration to licensing the technology to major brand name manufacturers (e.g., Black & Decker, Jacuzzi) and supply of components on an OEM basis. In this way, we can pursue total industry dominance for the foreseeable future.

The company recognizes that its product falls into a niche between two well-established industries: recreational swimming pool amenities and the residential alarm and security business. As such, the high end of the market provides the opportunity to create zero maintenance optional components for both of these industry channels to market to new pool contractors and residential security system sales and installation companies.

As a part of its marketing strategy, the company will attempt to work closely with the regional directors of the Consumer Product Safety Commission (CPSC) and other related safety interest groups to gain product endorsement. There is currently a growing fight between the CPSC and pool contractors as the government body is lobbying strongly for all pools to be fenced and secured as a part of standard building codes. This is being fought strenuously by the industry based on both economic and esthetic rationale. A logical compromise may be mutual agreement on a fail-safe pool intrusion alarm. Such a move would parallel the inclusion of smoke alarms in new home construction.

The three primary consumer motivations for purchase of a pool intrusion alarm are

(a) child safety

(b) security from unauthorized pool use

(c) pet safety

The company will target to achieve 20% market penetration on the in-ground pool market and 5% of above-ground pools within five years through direct manufacturing and distribution of its own in-house product line and expects that this will equal one-third of all ultrasonic immersion surveillance systems installed by 1995. In addition, to promote wide industry acceptance of this technology as the industry standard, the company will license established manufacturer/distributors to market brand name replicas of the ULC product line and supply key technical components along with licensing rights. It expects to net $20 per unit supplying components to three brand name assemblers encouraged to enter the market and secure licensing fees and royalties from these plus a major security system manufacturer who will wish to incorporate the technology into more far-reaching systems.

Based on an assumed average retail price of $220, the following table summarizes the net revenue stream expected from three distinct groups. The table is based on the following assumptions:

(a) By 1994, 28% of the projected 6 million pools in the United States (currently 4.5 million) will have ultrasonic surveillance systems to monitor unauthorized pool intrusion.

(b) This translates to total sales of 1,400,000 units within the industry.

(c) Technology users will include three medium-size licensed assemblers who will start selling in 1991, 1992, and 1993 respectively and will buy components from ULC. Jointly they will sell over 300,000 units through 1994.

(d) A major licensee will pay a front-end fee with minimum sales guarantees to license the technology and manufacture its own system in house. ULC will derive a royalty of $10 per unit sold from manufacturers and assemblers.

At this stage of market analysis, the above target projection cannot be justified by market studies. The critical element to gain wide acceptance of the technology will be prototype performance. Based on such performance and the known mood of the industry and many consumer lobbyists toward child safety, the described strategy is simply a starting point to define the economic potential of the ultrasonic pool surveillance system.

The company has not yet analyzed the full potential of the spa market for a similar intrusion unit. While hot tubs and spas are often governed by the same building codes and bylaws, they are not generally perceived as having the same hazard level as pools. With their growing popularity and a number of recorded child drownings, this perception could change and/or consumer safety groups could soon place more emphasis on the need for spa security. Ultimately, then, a more compact version of the Lifeguard One could become a lucrative product spinoff to satisfy this market.

The following table summarizes the number of projected unit sales in the first five years that the technology is available to the marketplace.

PROJECTED ULTRASONIC POOL INTRUSION ALARM SALES OVER A FIVE-YEAR PERIOD BY ALL LICENSED MANUFACTURER/DISTRIBUTORS ($)

MARKETER	1990	1991	1992	1993	1994
Ultrasonic Lifeguard Corporation	5,000	20,000	100,000	200,000	360,000
Licensed assembler/ Distributors (3)		5,000	25,000	100,000	200,000
Licensed manufacturer			10,000	100,000	250,000
Total unit sales (1.4 million)	5,000	25,000	135,000	400,000	810,000

REVENUES ATTRIBUTABLE TO ABOVE UNIT PLACEMENTS
(Figures shown in $000s)

MARKETER	1990	1991	1992	1993	1994
ULC direct @ $120/unit	600	2,400	12,000	24,000	43,200
Assemblers—					
Components (net)		100	500	2,000	4,000
License fee		100	100	100	
Royalty		50	250	1,000	2,000
Manufacturer					
License fee			500		
Royalty			100	1,000	2,500
Total revenues	600	2,650	13,450	28,100	51,700

The Financial Plan

ULC has estimated its financial needs on the basis of three major levels of investment risk and, as a result, are determined to enlist funding support in three stages over the next 24 months. Ideally, the first stage financial partner will have the capability of funding the second stage, preparation for the initial product run in mid-1990. The full funding third stage will be tied to initial full-scale production in 1991 and the expected major expansion in 1992. To place our financial plan in perspective, we offer the following overview of requirements and expected achievements during the three phases of equity financing.

1) Stage One funding will allow the founders to present a complete technical prototype and five production prototypes of the Lifeguard One pool intrusion alarm. It will allow ULC marketing to arrange key demonstration and test sites for the prototypes and initiate talks with major regional distributors. It will provide the means of getting product certification from Underwriter Laboratories and, ideally, the endorsement of the Consumer Product Safety Commission. A full production strategy will evolve during this phase.

The estimated time frame is nine months from funding to achieve these goals and prepare for the initial production run. Total budget is set at $150,000. The major uncontrollable element is the time required to gain certification before embarking on the second stage. Allocation of the $150,000 may be summarized as follows:

Development equipment	$11,000
Computer and software	5,000
Telephone	2,000

Development retainer	$ 12,000
Production engineer	8,000
UL listing (including travel)	6,000
Government interaction	5,000
Retainer — S. Starnes	9,000
Market development	8,000
Retainer — R. Touchie	9,000
Creation of five beta units	10,000
Product field testing	10,000
General administrative expense	5,000
Production coordination	15,000
Trade show preparation	10,000
Unallocated funds	25,000
	$150,000

2) Stage Two is expected to have a financial need of $450,000 and will include the initial production and distribution of 1,000 units with focus exclusively in west coast states. Realistically, the company can expect minor product modifications as a result of early installations and wishes to concentrate all sales within a manageable territory for a small company. All sales support services, operational processes, and staff training will be aimed at developing a national distribution network in the last half of this nine-month phase. A second placement of 1,000 units is expected in the second half of this phase as the company prepares for full-scale national distribution. Estimated cash needs for this second segment of the first phase are $350,000 and this is illustrated as the opening cash position in Table 1 at the beginning of the actual manufacturing process. Production and assembly of YR1 units will be completed in the Pacific Northwest while plans are made to determine the most cost-effective mass production point for ensuing units.

3) Stage Three will focus on production planning and marketing as well as the development of new product models. The company expects to gear up to handle monthly volumes growing from 2,000 to 30,000 units over the first three years of full production. There are numerous alternative strategies that may be employed at this point. They range from startup of a U.S.-based production facility to off-shore manufacturing to acquisition of a complementary company with well-established distribution and production operations. All financial strategy related to these options will be developed with the company's financial partner. The projected cash need of $1,000,000 is based on renting an interim assembly facility to meet 1992 production needs.

Once the product line is established, a further $2,000,000 will be required to meet product demand and establish an effective corporate operational base in the ideal geographic location. This may prove to be a logical time for the company to pursue institutional or public investment as profitability and management performance will be established. Also it would allow for early investors to have a means of equity liquidation. Beyond this point, it is expected that ongoing financing can be provided through retained earnings and debt financing as required.

It is management's opinion that the long-term success of this venture is totally dependent on the successful design and introduction of the product in the first two phases. Income forecasts beyond 1992 depend on adequate and timely funding for product and market development.

Corporate Income Forecasts

The following forecasts are provided to demonstrate the economic incentives that have attracted management to this development project. THE COMPANY MAKES NO REPRESENTATION THAT THE PROJECTIONS WILL BE ACHIEVED OR THAT THE ASSUMPTIONS ON WHICH THEY ARE BASED WILL REMAIN CONSTANT.

Table 1 is a Corporate Five-year Financial Forecast and isolates corporate operating profit from its internal production process as well as the expected development of revenues from industry members licensed to market products using patented ULC technology. Because investment tax credits and research and development tax credits will vary with the source of financing, their implications have been omitted from the projections and will be discussed individually with interested parties.

Table 2 provides a summary of the projected production and marketing budgets to achieve target revenue goals.

Management wishes to emphasize that a part of the start-up procedure for this company will be the creation of detailed cost accounting systems and report creation. This will enable us not only to oversee day-to-day activity, but will provide an effective communication base for our financial partner.

The company plans to review and update its financial forecasts at the end of Phase One and Phase Two and will provide regular financial data to the Board of Directors. It is intended that the senior financial partner will be a member of the board.

TABLE 1
ULTRASONIC LIFEGUARD CORPORATION
CORPORATE PROFIT AND CASH FLOW FORECASTS
(Figures shown in $000s)

	YR1	YR2	YR3	YR4	YR5
Operating profit —					
Direct production	30	312	3,300	8,160	17,880
License fees/royalties	-	250	1,450	4,100	8,500
Gross operating profit	30	560	4,750	12,260	26,380
Corporate overhead	150	300	450	750	1,200
Net operating profit	(120)	260	4,300	11,510	25,180

	YR1	YR2	YR3	YR4	YR5
Opening cash position*	350	1,010	2,480	2,720	7,760
Operating cash —					
Net outflow	100				
Net inflow		50	2,600	8,000	20,000
Application to —					
Product development	120	240	360	480	600
Market development *	120	240	360	480	600
Closing cash position	10	480	4,320	9,760	26,560
Additional cash needs (investment)	1,000	2,000	(1,600)	(2,000)	

* Opening cash position assumes the infusion of Phase One and Phase Two of Development of $600,000 prior to the generation of revenue in the first year of sales (1990). The company isolates its investment in product and market development as non-operating cash outflow so as to accurately measure the efficiency of operating profit centers.

Only payback of original investment is illustrated and excess cash applications will depend on dividend policy and existing expansion opportunities for the company. The variation in profit and cash flow is based on the expected asset build-up and its related cash requirements.

TABLE 2
DIRECT MANUFACTURING AND SALES
(Figures shown in $000s)

	YR1	YR2	YR3	YR4	YR5
Revenue	600	2,400	12,000	24,000	43,000
Cost of goods sold:					
Materials & labor	150	600	3,000	6,000	10,800
Direct sales	90	360	1,800	3,600	6,480
Gross profit	360	1,690	8,650	18,500	34,420
Manufacturing overhead	120	432	1,800	2,880	3,288
Marketing overhead	150	480	1,200	1,920	2,592
Operations administration	60	216	900	1,440	2,160
Total fixed costs*	330	1,128	3,900	6,240	8,040
Operating profit	30	462	4,750	12,260	28,380

* Direct materials are projected at 25% of wholesale price and direct marketing commissions and costs are estimated at 15%.

Overheads will decline to 15.5% of product revenues in the fifth year. Economies of scale will lead to percentage reductions in all three overhead areas as the company grows: manufacturing falls from 20% to 9% over five years, marketing from 25% to 6%, administration from 10% to 5%.

These projections assume that the company will subcontract most component production and function primarily as an assembly facility and distribution center for North America.

While corporate policy will include a steady growth of product and market development activity, the revenue projections do not include any spinoff products which might result from this effort. Only revenues related to the assumed penetration of the pool alarm market are included in these estimates. It is expected that by the third operating year the company will invest in its own assembly plant, likely in a sunbelt state.

The Team

The three founders of ULC offer a combined experience and knowledge base appropriate to the founding of the company. Their complementary backgrounds will serve the company's general management, product development, and sales management requirements during its first two years of operation. Support management in the manufacturing and administrative areas will be added as required. The general manager is well versed in recruiting and administering the human resource needs of development companies.

The company's product development force is Robert L. Mills, formerly with IBM and then one of Lockheed Missile's most decorated electronic technicians over a 10-year period. At Lockheed, Mr. Mills' inventive capacity was renowned as he received 135 separate Engineering Excellence Awards during his employment (four times more than any other Lockheed engineer had ever accomplished). For the past 20 years, Bob Mills has been an independent design consultant with a unique knowledge base covering many aspects of electronics and physics. He has designed and invented numerous components for everything from missiles to swimming pool computerized filtering systems.

Elaine Tanner, a former Olympic swimmer, is an energetic entrepreneur with a proven sales record and established credentials as a profit-maker. She is the company's main liaison with regulatory bodies and has developed an international network of production and distribution channels while operating as an importer/exporter during the last eight years. Ms. Tanner will lead the company's sales effort.

General management is in the hands of Rodger Touchie, B.Comm. (Finance), MBA (Marketing), with 20 years of related experience and a history of successful team management in technology and development companies. Mr. Touchie's balanced expertise in the financial and marketing areas allows the company to minimize executive overheads as we define both our marketing strategies and operational cost controls.

The company's internal team is supplemented by external professional services including a national firm of patent attorneys, an established production design consultant, and pending two individuals currently employed as senior sales staff in the swimming pool industry.

With the investment process the company hopes to add to its board of directors two experienced business professionals who can play an active role in defining long-term corporate goals.

The names and detailed backgrounds of the above personnel are available to potential investors on a confidential basis.

Conclusion

Approximately 15 months ago, 20/20, the highly successful TV news show, aired a 15-minute segment showing the horrible reality of child drowning. In June 1989, it was repeated with an update and the comment that they would likely air their concerns at the beginning of every summer for the next decade. In the field of immersion alarm systems, they had nothing new to report in 1989.

Taking a technical product from the conceptual stage to the production stage is often fraught with peril. However, while we do not wish to understate the inherent investment risk of this venture, there are some aspects to this project that are unique. All of the technologies to be integrated in the design are well tested and offer minimal technical uncertainty. Until the company's patent application was made, no individual had integrated these electronic elements and applied them to this field. Ultrasonic depth sounders, infrared detectors, motion sensors all have their place, but in terms of guarding a swimming pool from unwanted entry, the company's product design stands well above all other known options.

Ultrasonic's management team is confident that, with proper investment support, we can deliver a quality product that is both socially redeemable and full of profit potential.

APPENDIX 2
MANAGEMENT ACCOUNTING STATEMENT FORMATS FOR THE HOTEL INDUSTRY USING THE UNIFORM SYSTEM OF ACCOUNTS

Periodically you will be called on to provide financial summaries for your board of directors, banker, investors, or potential investors. There are two types of useful financial statements.

Most common are the publicly distributed annual statements prepared by an external accountant according to generally accepted accounting principles. They are particularly good for situations in which you need to disclose financial data while giving a limited insight into the real workings of the company.

The second set is based either on supplemental reports prepared by the external auditor or internally generated statements used primarily in the management process.

At one time, I was involved in the acquisition and management of the Sheraton Marina Inn, Corpus Christi, Texas, and had worked with a range of hotel industry statement formats. In this industry, standardized statement formats have evolved over time to a more advanced point than most industries. The following information is included to give some insight into statement format options and is provided only as a guideline to help develop your own general ledger accounts and statement formats.

The information is divided into three parts:

(a) The Summary of Hotel Operating Results is a brief report that shows an external accountant's schedule of monthly net room revenue and summary of operations, plus a summary operating budget for the following year. (See pages 154 to 157.)

(b) The second set of statements, Comparative Operating Results, was used later to illustrate progress for a planned refinancing and property expansion. (See pages 158 to 161.)

(c) The final group shows a selection of data from financial statements used to evaluate the hotel prior to acquisition. (See pages 162 to 175.)

Note: This property was subsequently sold and these reproductions are in no way meant to reflect upon current ownership or management.

SHERATON CORPUS CHRISTI INN
Schedule of monthly net room revenues

For the year ended December 31, 199-

January	$193,126.16
February	210,082.16
March	240,284.80
April	233,386.75
May	245,044.49
June	261,526.50
July	287,020.91
August	270,993.50
September	256,750.76
October	234,377.84
November	216,958.55
December	164,728.25
	$2,814,280.67

See accompanying notes to schedule of monthly net room revenues.

SHERATON CORPUS CHRISTI INN
Summary of Operations
For the year ended December 31, 199-
(Unaudited) (Figures shown in $)

	Revenue	Cost of revenue	Payroll and related expense	Other expense	Gross profit
Operating departments:					
Rooms	2,814,280	—	435,336	125,398	2,253,546
Telephone	160,911	116,924	19,216	35,569	(10,798)
Newsstand	5,623	5,542	—	5	76
Food and beverage	1,796,806	582,001	506,069	314,117	394,619
Other	15,531	—	—	7,733	7,798
	4,793,151	704,467	960,621	482,822	2,645,241
Indirect expense:					
Administrative and general	—	—	118,945	313,554	432,499
Advertising and sales promotion	—	—	43,965	83,089	127,054
Heat, light, and power	—	—	—	216,226	216,226
Repairs and maintenance	—	—	95,654	180,153	275,807
	—	—	258,564	793,022	1,051,586
House revenue, expense and operating profit	4,793,151	704,467	1,219,185	1,275,844	1,593,655
Occupancy cost:					
Management fee				235,875	
Insurance				23,833	
Interest				597,227	
Real estate taxes				68,360	
Other				61,467	986,762
Net profit from operations before depreciation					$606,893

SHERATON CORPUS CHRISTI INN
199- Operating Budget
(Figures shown in $)

	Jan.	Feb.	Mar.	Apr.	May	June	July	Aug.	Sept.	Oct.	Nov.	Dec.	TOTAL
REVENUE													
Rooms	236,000	241,570	283,210	274,050	283,210	309,256	319,548	302,746	292,950	302,746	227,850	201,810	3,274,936
Food													
Spanish Main & Banquets	64,860	73,310	80,350	80,160	80,800	73,720	80,810	85,940	85,170	85,590	66,750	97,060	954,520
Bella Fonte	24,140	26,260	30,340	29,320	28,590	29,500	30,750	29,980	25,100	25,610	24,200	28,850	332,640
Beverage													
Spanish Main & Banquets	30,380	32,150	34,300	32,280	31,250	33,500	37,300	37,160	36,250	38,650	27,220	42,120	412,560
Bella Fonte	14,740	17,060	20,550	19,700	27,760	24,750	25,200	22,200	20,140	20,170	19,260	18,340	249,870
Telephone	10,670	10,910	12,790	12,380	12,790	13,070	13,510	12,790	12,380	12,790	9,630	8,530	142,240
Newsstand	410	420	490	470	490	500	520	490	470	490	370	330	5,450
Other income	1,280	1,280	1,280	1,400	1,280	1,280	1,280	1,400	1,280	1,280	1,280	1,400	15,720
Total revenue	382,480	402,960	463,310	449,760	466,170	485,576	508,918	492,706	473,740	487,326	376,560	398,440	5,387,936
DEPARTMENT EXPENSES													
Rooms	46,480	47,330	53,720	52,160	53,720	55,300	56,720	54,380	53,050	54,380	43,560	39,570	610,370
Food													
Spanish Main & Banquets	47,290	52,380	57,500	57,230	57,360	53,080	57,370	61,080	60,710	60,520	47,930	68,820	681,270
Bella Fonte	24,720	26,210	30,240	29,060	27,470	28,890	29,280	28,760	25,150	24,990	24,010	28,210	326,990
Beverage													
Spanish Main & Banquets	18,000	18,130	19,290	18,680	18,320	19,050	20,330	20,300	19,940	20,750	17,150	21,940	231,880
Bella Fonte	8,320	8,990	10,610	9,770	13,830	12,740	12,750	11,310	10,490	9,900	9,640	9,960	128,310
Telephone	11,600	11,750	12,910	12,650	12,910	13,080	13,350	12,910	12,650	12,910	10,960	10,290	147,970
Newsstand	270	270	320	310	320	330	340	320	310	320	240	210	3,560
Total department expense	156,680	165,060	184,590	179,860	183,930	182,470	190,140	189,060	182,300	183,770	153,490	179,000	2,130,340
DEPARTMENTAL PROFIT	225,800	237,900	278,720	269,900	282,240	303,106	318,778	303,646	291,440	303,556	223,070	219,440	3,257,596

OPERATING BUDGET — Continued
(Figures shown in $)

	Jan.	Feb.	Mar.	Apr.	May	June	July	Aug.	Sept.	Oct.	Nov.	Dec.	TOTAL
Indirect expenses													
Administrative & general	35,380	35,910	38,480	37,910	38,530	40,180	42,040	41,110	40,420	41,020	36,300	35,500	462,830
Advertising & sales	12,270	12,270	12,270	12,270	12,270	12,270	12,750	12,750	12,750	12,750	12,750	12,750	150,120
Heat, light, & power	17,480	17,860	20,660	20,060	20,650	21,000	21,810	20,660	20,060	20,660	19,620	16,760	237,280
Repairs & maintenance	19,560	19,560	19,560	19,560	19,560	19,560	20,340	20,340	20,340	20,340	20,340	20,340	239,400
Total indirect expenses	84,690	85,600	90,970	89,800	91,010	93,010	96,940	94,860	93,570	94,770	89,010	85,400	1,089,630
HOUSE PROFIT	141,110	152,300	187,750	180,100	191,230	210,096	221,838	208,786	197,870	208,786	134,060	134,040	2,167,966
Capital expenses													
Rent, taxes, & insurance	12,900	14,200	14,650	16,870	16,190	16,820	15,400	15,400	16,400	15,400	15,400	16,400	186,030
Management fee	19,120	20,150	23,160	22,490	23,300	24,280	25,460	24,630	23,690	24,370	18,830	19,920	269,400
NET OPERATING INCOME	109,090	117,950	149,940	140,740	151,740	168,996	180,978	168,756	157,780	169,016	99,830	97,720	1,712,536
Debt service — flats note													
Interest	46,710	46,500	46,290	46,080	45,870	45,650	45,440	45,220	45,000	44,770	44,550	44,320	546,400
Principal	24,990	25,200	25,410	25,620	25,840	26,050	26,270	26,500	26,710	26,930	27,160	27,380	314,060
Investors' distribution	37,500	37,500	37,500	37,500	37,500	37,500	37,500	37,500	37,500	37,500	37,500	37,500	450,000
NET CASH FLOW	-110	8,750	40,740	31,540	42,530	59,796	71,768	59,536	48,570	59,816	-9380	-11,480	
Cumulative		8,640	49,380	80,920	123,450	183,246	255,014	314,550	363,120	422,936	413,556	402,076	
Net operating income	109,090	117,950	149,940	140,740	151,740	168,996	180,978	168,756	157,780	169,016	99,830	97,720	1,712,536
Less interest	46,710	46,500	46,290	46,080	45,870	45,650	45,440	45,220	45,000	44,770	44,550	44,320	546,400
Net income (loss)	62,380	71,450	103,650	94,660	105,870	123,346	135,538	123,536	112,780	124,246	55,280	53,400	1,166,136

SHERATON CORPUS CHRISTI INN
Comparative operating results for the 12 months ending October 31, 199- and October 31, 199-

	12 months to Oct. 31/9-	12 months to Oct. 31/9-
Occupancy	84.8%	78.9%
Average room rate	$50.18	$59.85
Revenue		
Rooms	$2,717,896	$2,984,554
Food	1,089,177	1,192,096
Beverage	539,681	589,225
Telephone	136,884	135,014
Newsstand	5,623	6,434
Other income	15,890	21,060
Total	4,505,151	4,928,383
Cost of sales		
Food	419,704	380,161
Beverage	120,651	119,709
Telephone	128,820	121,635
Total	669,175	621,505
Gross profit	3,835,976	4,306,878
Department expenses		
Rooms	554,017	568,988
Food	591,684	554,741
Beverage	234,718	205,693
Telephone	18,699	20,147
Newsstand	5,880	4,551
Total	1,404,998	1,354,120
Department profit	2,430,978	2,952,758
Indirect expenses		
Administrative & general	426,772	430,286
Advertising & sales	137,276	127,881
Heat, light, & power	208,297	244,546
Repairs & maintenance	214,724	247,164
Total	987,069	1,049,877
House profit	1,443,909	1,902,881
Property expenses		
Rent	23,623	46,338
Taxes	65,483	64,655
Insurance	21,333	27,731
Total	110,439	138,724
Net operating income	$1,333,470	$1,764,157

SHERATON CORPUS CHRISTI INN
Rooms department operating results for the years ending October 31, 199- and October 31, 199-

	Year ending Oct. 31/9-		Year ending Oct. 31/9-	
Room revenue	$2,717,896	100.0%	$2,984,554	100.0%
Department expenses				
Salaries & wages	$367,493	13.5%	$342,677	11.8%
Payroll taxes & benefits	66,750	2.5%	76,318 (1)	2.5%
Cleaning supplies	13,326	0.5%	13,573	0.5%
Commissions (travel agents)	15,895	0.6%	23,151	0.8%
Guest supplies	29,088	1.1%	37,096 (2)	1.2%
Laundry	7,818	0.3%	6,841	0.2%
Reservations expense	21,226	0.8%	24,941	0.8%
Uniforms	6,442	0.2%	5,544	0.2%
Linen	14,771	0.5%	24,933 (2)	0.8%
Stationery & supplies	2,722	0.1%	9,668 (2)	0.3%
Pest control	1,336	—	1,646	—
Window cleaning	7,150	0.2%	2,600	=
Total	554,017	20.4%	568,988	19.1%
Department profit	$2,163,879	79.6%	$2,415,566	80.9%

Notes:

1. Increase in benefits cost due to enhanced employee group insurance plan.

2. Guest supplies, linens, and stationery expense increases reflect the room and amenities upgrade program started in early 199-.

SHERATON CORPUS CHRISTI INN
Food department operating results for the years ending October 31, 199- and October 31, 199-

	Year ending Oct. 31/9-		Year ending Oct. 31/9-	
Revenue	$1,089,177	100.0%	$1,192,096	100.0%
Food cost	419,704	38.5%	380,161	31.9%
Gross profit	669,473	61.5%	811,935	68.1%
Department expenses				
Salaries & wages	$432,962	39.9%	$400,699	33.6%
Payroll taxes & benefits	75,404	6.9%	89,153	7.4%
China, glass, & silver	13,123	1.2%	12,111	1.0%
Cleaning supplies	10,557	1.0%	13,369	1.1%
Guest supplies	13,808	1.3%	7,903	0.7%
Laundry& linens	4,920	0.4%	6,626	0.6%
Licenses & permits	1,736	0.2%	3,361	0.3%
Menu & drink list	3,607	0.3%	1,867	0.2%
Educational expense	1,987	0.2%	885	—
Music & entertainment	4,646	0.4%	1,252	0.1%
Promotion	9,249	0.8%	3,451	0.3%
Uniforms	6,869	0.6%	5,081	0.4%
Utensils & small appliances	2,972	0.3%	2,252	0.2%
Office supplies	3,536	0.3%	1,863	0.2%
Pest control	2,210	0.2%	3,393	0.3%
Banquet expense	1,431	0.1%	1,200	0.1%
General	2,667	0.2%	275	—
Total	591,684	54.3%	554,741	46.5%
Department profit	$77,789	7.2%	$257,194	21.6%

SHERATON CORPUS CHRISTI INN
Beverage department operating results
for years ending October 31, 199- and October 31, 199-

	Year ending Oct. 31/9-		Year ending Oct. 31/9-	
Revenue	$539,681	100.0%	$589,225	100.0%
Beverage cost	120,651	22.4%	119,709	20.3%
Gross profit	$419,030	77.6%	$469,516	79.7%
Department expenses				
Salaries & wages	$81,685	15.2%	$79,511	13.5%
Payroll taxes & benefits	11,015	2.0%	16,321	2.8%
Licenses & permits	2,316	0.4%	7,753	1.3%
Bar expense	19,903	3.7%	18,004	3.1%
China, glass, & silver	2,914	0.5%	4,926	0.8%
Guest supplies	8,062	1.5%	6,800	1.2%
Music	100,690	18.7%	65,447	11.1%
Fees & permits	3,238	0.6%	1,502	0.3%
Travel & entertainment	1,192	0.2%	566	0.1%
Uniforms	3,646	0.7%	4,005	0.7%
General	57	—	858	0.1%
Total	234,718	43.5%	205,693	35.0%
Department profit	$184,312	34.1%	$263,823	44.7%

SHERATON CORPUS CHRISTI INN
ASSETS
(Figures shown in $)

	September 30 199-	September 30 199-
Current assets		
Cash		
House funds	3,025	3,025
Corpus Christi National Bank		
Operating account	78,929	28,465
Petty cash account	1,199	1,199
Package store account	13,909	11,957
Payroll account	55,615	65,020
Savings account	239,646	428,768
Mercantile National Bank		
MasterCard	48,750	166,905
	441,073	705,339
Accounts receivable (note 1)		
Guest ledger	12,413	14,738
City ledger	114,270	70,559
Employees	—	1,296
Other	14,368	3,030
Federal income tax refund	64,386	—
	205,437	89,623
Less allowance for doubtful accounts	2,750	2,642
	202,687	86,981
Inventories of merchandise		
(lower of cost or market, on first in, first out basis)	32,242	30,182
Prepaid expenses		
Insurance	66,071	88,800
Advertising	—	3,383
Other	905	8,412
	66,976	100,595
Total current assets	742,978	923,097
Advances to stockholder	62,500	—
Furniture, fixtures, and equipment, at cost (note 1)	480,045	137,200
Less accumulated depreciation	86,134	22,040
	393,911	115,160
Other assets		
Deposits	380	380
	1,199,769	1,038,637

See notes to financial statements

SHERATON CORPUS CHRISTI INN
LIABILITY AND STOCKHOLDERS' EQUITY
(Figures shown in $)

	Year ended September 30	
	199-	199-
Current liabilities		
Note payable (note 2)	23,139	23,139
Accounts payable		
Trade	7,576	29,656
Other	4,168	8,497
	11,744	38,153
Taxes payable and accrued		
Federal income taxes (note 1)	—	56,437
Payroll	11,798	10,980
Sales and occupancy	39,612	35,693
Real estate and personal property	45,908	44,199
	97,318	147,309
Accrued expenses		
Salaries and wages	30,545	29,332
Bonuses (note 1)	102,218	110,868
Management fee (note 6)	26,304	—
Utilities	—	5,374
Other	14,307	18,037
	173,374	163,611
Total current liabilities	305,575	372,212
Long-term debt (note 2)	—	23,139
Advances by stockholder	—	10,390
Commitments (note 3)		
Stockholders' equity		
Common stock, $1 par value; authorized, 1,000,000 shares; issued and outstanding, 1,000 share	1,000	1,000
Retained earning	893,194	631,896
	1,199,796	1,038,637

SHERATON CORPUS CHRISTI INN
STATEMENT OF INCOME AND RETAINED EARNINGS
(Figures shown in $)

	Year ended September 30	
	199-	199-
Revenues		
Rooms	1,818,301	1,649,357
Food	833,730	784,255
Beverage	239,263	256,455
Telephone	119,902	117,361
Newsstand	39,878	36,256
Package store	17,214	16,812
Beauty salon	31,187	31,546
Miniature train	3,053	2,590
Other	61,827	26,920
	3,164,355	2,921,552
Cost of sales		
Food	333,941	292,123
Beverage	51,547	53,909
Telephone	114,255	113,819
Newsstand	31,441	27,809
Package store	11,865	11,814
Beauty salon	3,463	3,507
	546,512	502,981
Gross profit	2,617,843	2,418,571
Operating expenses		
Rooms	459,289	403,988
Food	396,629	351,977
Beverage	89,986	87,746
Telephone	14,028	14,978
Newsstand	7,311	6,367
Package store	1,348	1,144
Beauty salon	23,075	23,871
Miniature train	18,642	11,595
Administrative & general	461,632	439,556
Advertising & sales promotion	59,010	58,295
Heat, light, & power	142,779	145,947
Repairs & maintenance	176,757	151,852
	1,850,486	1,697,316
Capital expenses (note 5)	429,737	371,401

STATEMENT OF INCOME AND RETAINED EARNINGS — Continued

Income before provision for federal income taxes	337,620	349,854
Provision for federal income taxes (note 1)	76,322	140,708
Net income	261,298	209,146
Retained earnings beginning of year	631,896	422,750
Retained earnings end of year	893,194	631,896
Net income per share (note 4)	261	209

See notes to financial statements

SHERATON CORPUS CHRISTI INN
STATEMENT OF CHANGES IN FINANCIAL POSITION
(Figures shown in $)

	Year ended September 30	
	199-	199-
Source of working capital		
Operations		
Net income	261,298	209,146
Add item not affecting working capital		
Depreciation	64,094	13,116
Working capital provided by operations	325,392	222,262
Proceeds from borrowing	—	46,278
	325,392	268,540
Application of working capital		
Increase in advances to stockholder	62,500	—
Purchase of furniture, fixtures, & equipment	342,845	92,357
Current maturities of long-term debt	23,139	23,139
Reduction of amount due to stockholder	10,390	80,556
	438,874	196,052
Increase (decrease) in working capital	(113,482)	72,488
Increase (decrease) in components of working capital		
Cash	(264,266)	117,154
Accounts receivable	115,706	(12,125)
Inventories of merchandise	2,060	1,360
Prepaid expenses	(33,619)	64,005
Notes payable	(9,494)	(8,139)
Accounts payable	26,409	(14,141)
Taxes payable and accrued	49,991	(69,722)
Accrued expenses	(269)	(5,904)
Increase (decrease) in working capital	(113,482)	72,488

See notes to financial statements

SHERATON CORPUS CHRISTI INN
ROOMS

	Year ended September 30	
	199-	199-
Revenue		
Guest rooms revenue	$1,825,411	$1,656,312
Less allowances	7,110	6,955
	1,818,301	1,649,357
Expenses		
Salaries and wages	301,729	256,928
Bonuses	13,891	12,297
Employees' meals	12,132	6,143
Payroll taxes and employee benefits	34,813	28,980
Cleaning supplies	11,954	10,839
Commissions	8,356	7,996
Guest supplies	27,019	25,378
Linen & house laundry	20,265	24,584
Contract window cleaning	3,550	3,300
Music	1,214	1,090
Pest control	710	685
Printing & stationery	591	749
Reservation expense	14,398	13,363
Telephone expense	—	9
Uniforms	6,606	4,886
Office supplies	2,448	3,655
Miscellaneous	2,033	4,523
	461,709	405,405
Less expenses allocated to other departments	(2,420)	(1,417)
	459,289	403,988
Departmental income	$1,359,012	$1,245,369
Percentages		
Net revenue	100.0%	100.0%
Expenses		
Salaries & wages	16.5	15.6
Employees' meals	0.6	0.4
Payroll taxes and employee benefits	1.9	1.8
Cleaning supplies	0.6	0.7
Guest supplies	1.4	1.6
Linen & house laundry	1.1	1.5
All other expenses	3.1	2.9
	25.2	24.5
Departmental income	74.8%	75.5%

SHERATON CORPUS CHRISTI INN
ROOM STATISTICS

	Year ended September 30	
	199-	199-
Number of rooms available in hotel	175	175
Total rooms available for the year	63,875	63,875
Total rooms occupied	54,841	55,885
Percentage of rooms occupied	85.9%	87.5%
Rooms revenue — guest (net)	$1,818,301	$1,649,357
Number of guests	73,702	76,987
Average daily rate per occupied room	$33.16	$29.48
Average number of guests per occupied room	1.34	1.4

SHERATON CORPUS CHRISTI INN
FOOD
(Figures shown in $)

	Year ended September 30	
	199-	199-
Revenue		
Cafe Olé	248,841	246,118
Spanish Main	355,607	321,688
Room service	46,614	45,567
Banquets	170,334	162,647
	821,396	776,020
Less allowances	987	908
	820,409	775,112
Cost of sales		
Cost of food consumed	366,865	320,598
Less credit for employees' meals	32,924	28,475
	333,941	292,123
Gross profit on sales	486,468	482,989
Other income		
Public room rental (banquets)	13,321	9,143
Gross profit	499,789	492,132
Expenses		
Salaries & wages	297,876	249,910
Bonuses	10,855	13,635
Employees' meals	11,327	14,217
Payroll taxes & employee benefits	38,209	34,198
Banquet expenses	1,264	2,793
China, glass, & silver	4,652	12,435
Cleaning supplies	6,559	5,620
Guest supplies	7,734	6,453
Laundry & linen rental	7,004	2,716
Licenses & permits	180	748
Menus & beverage lists	1,385	758
Miscellaneous	2,427	1,688
Music & entertainment	1,952	1,115
Printing & stationery	—	438
Uniforms	2,515	3,517
Utensils	2,517	1,242
Contract cleaning	173	494
	396,629	351,977
Departmental income	103,160	140,155

FOOD — Continued

Percentages		
Revenue		
Food sales — net	100.0%	100.0%
Cost of sales		
Cost of food consumed	44.7	41.4
Less credit for employees' meals	4.0	3.7
	40.7	37.7
Gross profit on sales	59.3	62.3
Other income		
Public room rental (banquets)	1.6	1.2
Gross profit	60.9	63.5
Expenses		
Salaries & wages	36.3	32.2
Bonuses	1.3	1.8
Employees' meals	1.3	1.8
Payroll taxes and employee benefits	4.6	4.4
China, glass, & silver	0.5	1.6
Cleaning supplies	0.7	0.7
Laundry & linen rental	0.8	0.4
All other expenses	2.8	2.5
	48.3	45.4
Departmental income	12.6%	18.1%

SHERATON CORPUS CHRISTI INN
BEVERAGE

	Year ended September 30	
	199-	199-
Revenue		
Beverage service	$239,286	$256,614
Less allowances	23	159
Net revenue	239,263	256,455
Cost of beverage sold	51,547	53,909
Gross profit	187,716	202,546
Expenses		
Salaries & wages	27,063	24,137
Bonuses	6,010	8,057
Employees' meals	1,290	2,462
Payroll taxes and employee benefits	4,441	3,633
Bar expense	7,462	7,504
China, glass, & silver	2,155	2,398
Guest supplies	2,932	1,892
Music & entertainment	34,982	34,533
Miscellaneous	395	630
Uniforms	776	370
Licenses & permits	2,480	2,130
	89,986	87,746
Departmental income	$97,730	$114,800
Percentages		
Net revenue	100.0%	100.0%
Cost of beverage sold	21.5	22.2
Gross profit	78.5	77.8
Expenses		
Salaries & wages	14.4	9.4
Bonuses	3.2	3.2
Employees' meals	0.6	1.0
Payroll taxes & employee benefits	2.3	1.4
China, glass, & silver	1.1	0.9
Music & entertainment	18.6	13.5
All other expenses	7.7	3.7
	47.9	33.1
Departmental income	30.6%	44.7%

SHERATON CORPUS CHRISTI INN
TELEPHONE
(Figures shown in $)

	Year ended September 30	
	199-	199-
Revenue		
Local calls	13,425	13,972
Toll and long distance calls	88,164	85,947
Commissions — long distance calls	17,505	13,481
Commissions — pay station	818	3,962
Allowances	(10)	—
	119,902	117,362
Cost of calls		
Local calls	10,525	13,156
Toll and long distance	83,549	84,897
Equipment rental	20,181	15,766
	114,255	113,819
Gross profit	5,647	3,543
Operating expenses		
Salaries & wages	11,857	12,542
Bonuses	83	55
Employees' meals	568	723
Payroll taxes and employee benefits	1,520	1,658
	14,028	14,978
Departmental income (loss)	(8,381)	(11,435)

SHERATON CORPUS CHRISTI INN
ADMINISTRATIVE AND GENERAL
(Figures shown in $)

	Year ended September 30	
	199-	199-
Expenses		
Salaries & wages	108,692	90,592
Bonuses	62,184	66,236
Employees' meals	3,954	4,495
Payroll taxes and employee benefits	13,155	12,161
Cashiers' (overages) and shortages — net	230	(258)
Commissions on credit cards	41,715	40,097
Data processing	6,007	5,159
Dues & subscriptions	5,530	5,160
Franchise fees	51,473	49,481
Insurance general	25,105	20,079
Miscellaneous	5,644	5,771
Office supplies	6,945	6,338
Printing, postage, & stationery	2,821	2,160
Profit-sharing plan contribution	—	953
Professional fees	9,238	13,073
Provision for bad debts	2,200	9,500
Security expense	15,420	11,031
Telephone	1,680	1,602
Management fee	77,483	73,039
Travel & entertainment	4,833	5,266
Credit & collection	2,302	1,646
Contributions	11,231	13,870
Gasoline & automobile	3,790	2,105
Total administrative & general expenses	461,632	439,556

SHERATON CORPUS CHRISTI INN
ADVERTISING AND SALES PROMOTION
(Figures shown in $)

	Year ended September 30	
	199-	199-
Expenses		
Salaries & wages	31,713	28,116
Bonuses	4,063	4,404
Employees' meals	1,193	1,654
Payroll taxes and employee benefits	4,154	3,667
Dues & subscriptions	989	838
Guest certificates	—	480
Miscellaneous	1,494	2,147
Newspaper & magazine publications	9,016	9,472
Printing, postage, & stationery	1,887	3,496
Telephone	1,940	1,882
Travel & entertainment	2,561	2,139
Total advertising & sales promotion expenses	59,010	58,295

SHERATON CORPUS CHRISTI INN
HEAT, LIGHT, AND POWER
(Figures shown in $)

	Year ended September 30	
	199-	199-
Expenses		
Electricity	96,454	102,383
Electric bulbs & supplies	4,425	4,900
Fuel — gas	29,563	27,569
Water	7,618	7,829
Waste removal	4,719	3,266
Total heat, light, & power expenses	142,779	145,947

SHERATON CORPUS CHRISTI INN
REPAIRS AND MAINTENANCE
(Figures shown in $)

	Year ended September 30	
	199-	199-
Expenses		
Salaries & wages	70,083	56,164
Bonuses	2,211	2,265
Employees' meals	1,836	121
Payroll taxes and employee benefits	8,425	6,689
Building	35,329	30,560
Electrical & mechanical equipment	13,635	13,524
Furniture & furnishings	3,430	3,018
Grounds & landscaping	5,337	1,650
Educational expense	—	106
Television service	1,344	4,230
Painting & decorating	8,230	4,847
Swimming pool	1,806	1,433
Uniforms	918	459
Heating & air conditioning	11,206	14,850
Elevator	8,721	7,890
Engineering supplies	1,905	1,535
Auto expenses	2,341	2,511
Total repairs & maintenance expenses	176,757	151,852

SHERATON CORPUS CHRISTI INN
INSURANCE COVERAGE
September 30, 199-
(Figures shown in $)

CLASS OF RISK	AMOUNT OF INSURANCE COVERAGE
Fire and extended coverage (80% co-insurance)	
Building	4,000,000
Contents	1,000,000
Steam boiler and machinery	100,000
Plate glass — first floor	Scheduled
Innkeepers' liability (limit each guest)	50,000
Comprehensive catastrophe liability	5,000,000
Comprehensive general liability	
Bodily injury	500/500M
Property damage	500,000
Garage keepers' liability	120,000
Business interruption	692,000
Mixed beverage bond	7,500
Standard flood insurance	200,000
Comprehensive auto/garage liability	
Bodily injury	250/500M
Safe deposit box legal liability	200,000
Workers' compensation	Statutory

APPENDIX 3
OPERATIONAL MEMO

The following document represents a reprint of an actual recruiting memo used by a technology company to outline its sales and pricing strategy to potential executive sales representatives across North America.

Including such a summary as an appendix to your business plan illustrates a level of internal communication and documentation that speaks well for your management style. It helps prove that your business plan is more than words.

Because one of the primary concerns of investors lies in your approach to the marketplace, an operational memo such as this illustration is the best type of example to include. If you are not able to provide this, a similar internal summary of your management reporting system or production process and policies can be substituted.

U.S. SALES REPRESENTATION ORGANIZATIONAL DEVELOPMENT OUTLINE

The company's 1990 marketing program will aim at establishing sales representation in selected metropolitan markets in strategic locations around the country.

The implementation sequence will be determined by a variety of factors with the primary influence being the availability of suitable personnel to effectively enter first priority markets.

Product Policy — The golf simulator will initially be marketed as a turnkey system including a full one-year parts warranty and maintenance agreement plus two sets of golf clubs, Augusta National software, and the laser video disc production of the "World's Greatest Golf" series.

The available options will include a remote 24-inch monitor, 60-inch high-resolution screen, and an electronic payment system to provide user-activated machine time. Future options will include a dot matrix printer, RGB projection systems, and free-flight indoor models.

All units will be installed with an adequate supply of consumable parts (e.g., ball assembly) enclosed. National Support Corporation will represent our maintenance and service commitments in most areas of North America.

Pricing Policy — The basic retail price for the above-listed package is $31,800 U.S. However, the primary market for all company reps will be the commercial user, business operations who are employing the golf simulators as a profit generating device within their business environment. This customer base will receive commercial discounts ranging from 20% to 30% depending on the number of units purchased:

1 unit	$25,440
2 to 9 units	$23,840
10 or more units	$22,260

A secondary market will be wholesalers who have access to regional market niches or multi-end user customer groups and plan to resell the units. While the nature of specific situations may dictate special consideration as the need arises, these terms outline our general pricing policy:

2 to 9 units	$22,260
10 to 24 units	$20,680
25 to 99 units	$19,080
100 to 250 units	$17,480
250 or more units	$15,880

Note: Any and all potential wholesaler designations for specific customers must be cleared by Head Office before quoted.

Leasing Policy — On a national level we have made arrangements with TechLease Corporation whereby they have approved our system and arranged for coordination of lease applications through our head office. In most regions we expect that this program may be supplemented by regional lease companies who are more familiar with local businesses and therefore may be better qualified to expedite the lease application process. Rates are subject to change; at all times a current guideline may be to use a monthly rate factor of .0374 on all three-year quotes and .0290 on all four-year quotes.

A more detailed package including full contract terms will be available as required.

Introduction Policy — In each new market region the company rep will be allowed the opportunity to incentivize his or her initial customer by offering the wholesale price to his or her first installation. Preference should be given to a lead customer who will commit to the immediate purchase of two units minimum for this installation. A three-month option to expand initial purchase orders at this special price will be offered to your lead regional customer with head office approval under most conditions. Retail commission structure will apply on this sale and head office will allocate $1,000 per machine for co-op promotion with the lead customer.

We recommend that reps negotiate directly with this customer to ensure access to machines by other potential customers in the region as this will become your primary demo site.

Promotion Policy — The company plans to develop corporate sponsored promotions aimed at enhancing the popularity of the machines. A well-known professional will act as our national spokesperson. At this time, such programs are under development. Any suggestions for regional or national promotions should be directed to Head Office.

Corporate promotional support will come in the form of a concerted effort to develop broad trade coverage of our new technology and participation in a select group of regional and national trade expositions. Any suggestions in this area are welcome as the final 1990 agenda is not yet completed.

In addition, our Marketing Group is making a concerted effort to collect end user information from various market niches so as to provide both promotional guidance and useful documentation that we can apply to future sales efforts. All field reps will be expected to assist in this data collection process and ongoing customer support programs.

Personnel Policy — Lead candidates in each region must possess a balance of management potential, common sense, flexibility, sound communication skills, a consistent solid work ethic, integrity, willingness to represent the company interest in all corporate matters, and, in the grand tradition of salesmanship, they must exhibit the innate ability to close deals.

Most territories will be selected based on their market scope, eventually requiring two or three reps. The initial company sales representative would be the most likely person to assume territorial management responsibility. The likelihood over a period of three years is that territories will be consolidated into six major regions of the country with regional managers graduating from the territorial ranks.

Remuneration Policy — The primary incentive to this sales performance oriented network will be commissions earned. Given the pricing structure of the equipment and the availability of excellent leasing options for qualified customers, we foresee average sales incomes in the $50,000 to $60,000 range for the first full year. The following strategy is currently in place:

1. Once a lead candidate is identified, Head Office will provide a period of grace for him or her to establish the first customer using the sales tools readily available, including product videos, corporate brochures, pricing and leasing data, etc. At this time we cannot assure the availability of a demo machine in the immediate proximity while this effort is undertaken. Terms of sale for the first installation, as described above, should assist this effort.

2. Performance of the above will give us a reasonable level of comfort in offering the following package of commitments over the first six months of a formal relationship. Unless otherwise required by local law or tax requirements, we will prefer to establish an independent agency relationship with members of our sales force as we feel this provides mutual administrative advantages. The following points are relevant:

- (a) We will establish a conservative start-up budget for the region which will include $2,000 funding for phone installation, letterhead, business cards, direct promotional mailings, set mailing address in packaged office complex, etc.
- (b) Head office will supply all available support literature and an 800-line for easy communication.
- (c) A transportation, promotional, and monthly expense allowance will be jointly set based on the rep's application and business plan.
- (d) A monthly draw against commission will be negotiated based on circumstance and initial performance.
- (e) Commissions on all sales to commercial users will be calculated at 6% of sales on all 1990 orders fulfilled, due and payable 15 days after customer payment. In following years a quota will be established and monthly commissions will be graduated with a commission structure ranging from 4% to 7% of sales depending on levels of performance.

Note: All commissions on wholesale sales will be one half the rate of commercial user sales.

Note: In all cases it is expected that reps will place a minimum of 40 units per year and at an average unit selling price of $25,000 including accessories. This translates to a $1,000,000 sales target with resulting $60,000 commissions and the unnamed benefits of joining our Platinum Club (a sales achievement group that will be entitled to additional rewards and benefits currently undefined).

Sales Organization Growth Policy — As territories and regions grow, managers will be appointed to oversee all area sales activity and administer corporate policies and programs. It is our desire to work toward a system with limited red tape and administrative time so that sales managers will always maintain their own client base while supporting their sales force.

Our expectation is that the manager would always earn overrides on territorial sales and his or her earnings base would grow accordingly. However, it would be premature to set fixed policies in this area now. The issue will be addressed in more detail at a later date.

Product Development Policy — Now that our technology is defined we view ourselves as a market-driven company that will rely heavily on its forces in the marketplace to pass on useful information aimed at expansion of our product base and options. Primarily we plan to add new World Famous golf courses to our program and thereby create a software aftermarket for all installations as well as provide a logical extension for existing facilities to expand the number of golf simulators in place as course options grow. We hope to add two to three new courses per year.

While the simulation system will open many doors to our sales force and will long be the main ingredient in our product package, we expect that new generations and variations of the system will offer broad growth into other markets over the next decade. In addition, we are considering potential international distribution opportunities where we might opt to represent offshore products where specific end user groups that we plan to service are the target market of these product groups.

The Sweetswing Interactive Golfer is at the leading edge of golf simulation technology and offers a unique entertainment and educational format that has repeatedly been endorsed by recreational and professional golfers as a sure winner. In truth, it will only succeed if a professional sales force takes the product into the marketplace and establishes it as the dominant computerized golfing system across North America.

It is not a product that would assume to replace the game of golf or its professionals. On the contrary, it is a tool that will enhance the personal enjoyment of the recreational golfer and provide an excellent teaching mechanism for the club professional golfer.

More than anything it is a marvelous business opportunity for all — sales people, business operators, educators, promoters, and golfers everywhere!

Curtis Palmer

Curtis Palmer,
President
SweetSwing Interactive Golf Corp.

OTHER TITLES IN THE SELF-COUNSEL BUSINESS SERIES

TELECOMMUTING: MANAGING OFF-SITE STAFF FOR SMALL BUSINESS

Lin Grensing-Pophal
Suggested retail price: US $16.95 / CDN $21.95

Does your business need more employees, but you don't have the office space to accommodate them? Does someone on your staff want to work from home? Do you want to promote a flexible work environment but fear losing profits?

Telecommuting may be the answer. It can help you manage distance workers with confidence, set up an effective training and evaluation program, and provide flexibility while keeping your business on track.

The book includes:

- Determining whether telecommuting is right for your company
- Assessing current and new telework candidates
- Training telemanagers and teleworkers
- Helping on-site staff to cope
- Communicating effectively
- Setting up the home office
- Measuring the success of your program
- Taking care of the legal details

MOTIVATING TODAY'S EMPLOYEES

Lin Grensing-Pophal
Suggested retail price: US $16.95 / CDN $21.95

When you are watching the bottom line, it is easy to forget how your employees are feeling about their jobs. But unproductive staff can be one of the biggest threats to that bottom line, as many business owners have discovered to their cost.

A favourable working environment combined with good worker benefits has eclipsed salaries as the prime concern of the work force. Here is a book that tackles the job-satisfaction issue head-on. It offers creative options that will help companies increase worker effectiveness.

This book will answer the following questions:

- How do I identify effective motivators?
- Why should my company establish job standards?
- Is it important to involve employees in goal setting and decision making?
- How do I know whether I am hearing what employees are really saying?
- How do I handle problem employees?
- What nonmonetary incentives will work for my employees?
- How can I give workers a sense of "ownership" of their jobs?

READY-TO-USE BUSINESS FORMS
Suggested retail price: $21.95

- ***Give your business a professional look***
- ***Save time and money...we've designed the forms for you***
- ***Impress your customers with your new image***

Running a small business and keeping it in order can be made much simpler if efficient systems are in place and paperwork is up-to-date. Standardized business forms go a long way toward establishing and maintaining those systems. *Ready-to-Use Business Forms* includes all the forms typically used by businesses in their day-to-day operations.

The sample forms in this handy book can be photocopied or printed as needed. Includes personnel, sales and marketing, bookkeeping, budget, memo, telephone, invoice, credit, message, inventory, and requisition forms.

Also includes forms in Word 6.0 format on PC disk.

Order Form

All prices are subject to change without notice. Books are available in book, department, and stationery stores. If you cannot buy the book through a store, please use this order form.

(Please print.)

Name ______________________________

Address ______________________________

Charge to: ☐ Visa ☐ MasterCard

Account number ______________________________

Validation Date ______________________________

Expiry date ______________________________

Signature ______________________________

YES, please send me:

_____ *Telecommuting: Managing Off-site Staff for Small Business*

_____ *Motivating Today's Employees*

_____ *Ready to-Use Business Forms with Disk*

Please add the following for postage and handling charges: $3.50 for one book; $4.00 for more than one book.

In Canada, 7% GST will be added.

In Washington, 7.8% sales tax will be added.

☐ Check here for a free catalogue.

IN THE USA

Please send your order to:

Self-Counsel Press
1704 N. State Street
Bellingham, WA 98225

IN CANADA

Please send your order to the nearest location:

Self-Counsel Press
1481 Charlotte Road
North Vancouver, BC V7J 1H1

Self-Counsel Press
4 Bram Court
Brampton, ON L6W 3R6

Visit our Web site at: *www.self-counsel.com*

PREPARING A SUCCESSFUL BUSINESS PLAN (01)